Behind the Lines:
What it *Really Takes* to Make It as an Actor

By Jordan Ancel

Published by Jordan Ancel International

ISBN: 978-0-615-86076-3

Publisher Contact: Info@BehindTheLinesBook.com

Warning — Disclaimer

Thank you to everyone who contributed their time, energy, expertise, and knowledge to this book. Without you, there would be no book, and no industry to write about.

And special thanks to my mom and dad for always supporting and encouraging my creative endeavors.

For Brianna, my talented and beautiful wife who is a constant source of love and inspiration.

What's Inside

Preface • *i*

My Life As an Actor (a.k.a. What *Not* to Do) • *3*

The Reps

Brianna Ancel, *VP, Clear Talent Group* • *19*
David Ziff, *Senior VP, CESD* • *37*
Bob McGowan, *McGowan Management* • *45*
Jerry Silverhardt, *Manager* • *51*
TJ Stein, *Stein Entertainment Group* • *67*

The Casting Directors

Mark Teschner, *General Hospital* • *73*
Scott David, *Criminal Minds* • *87*
Renita Gale Swaekauski, Commercials & Films • *97*

The Teachers

Scott Sedita, *Scott Sedita Acting Studios* • *113*
Anthony Meindl, *Anthony Meindl's Actor Workshop* • *125*
Brian Reise, *Brian Reise Acting Studio* • *137*
Patrick Day, *Young Actors Space* • *151*

The Actors

Kathrine Narducci, *The Sopranos, A Bronx Tale* • *163*
Shaun Brown, *Newsroom, True Blood, The First Family* • *179*
Hemky Madera, *Weeds, Rango, Caribe Road* • *199*
Jesse Heiman, *Character Actor & Pop Culture Icon* • *213*

Spotlight

Allison Burnett, *Writer, Producer, Director* • *223*
Paul Smith, *Top Headshot Photographer* • *229*
Clear Talent Group Young People's Department • *235*

Preface

I've always liked attention. Maybe because I was an only child, or maybe growing up in New York City helped mold my wild imagination, or maybe because my mother was a writer and an artist. Perhaps all of these together made me want to be in the spotlight. I was the class clown, the fast-talker that could get into, and out of, any situation. I loved pretending and performing ever since I could talk. I wanted to be Han Solo.

I attended public school from kindergarten until high school, and then went to a state university. I was fortunate that I was in accelerated-learning programs, and equally lucky that my parents always nurtured my creativity. I excelled in art, so naturally, my parents encouraged me to take the entrance test for the very prestigious LaGuardia High School.

Back in the Early '80s, two major art schools combined into one. When High School for the Performing Arts, or PA, and Music and Art High School, or M&A merged, they moved to a new modern building in the shadows of Lincoln Center. The new unified school provided young artists and performers the best academic education while supporting and nurturing their creativity. Remember the movie (and subsequent remake) *Fame?* That was literally my high school.

Although strong in academics, the school was designed to foster artists, and I majored in fine art— graphic design, painting, illustration— but I always hung out with the actors, dancers, and singers.

I should mention now, that my school did not allow students to take classes in disciplines outside their field— artists couldn't sing, singers couldn't dance, etc.

However, I did perform quite a bit. But it was usually in math class or A.P. literature, where I often met with unfavorable reviews from the teachers. I also cut almost the entire semester of Art History during the beginning of my senior year because I wanted to attend the Gospel Chorus class with my best friend, Ali, and more importantly, the über-hot Kara was in Gospel Chorus, so I very much wanted to be there as often as possible.

It wasn't until discussion of the spring concert began, and

Ms. Del Valle, our lovely teacher, was going to give me the first solo bit in Verde's *Requiem*, that a disgruntled singing student in class ratted me out. So back to art history I went. Hey, I have perfect pitch, so it wasn't my fault I had gotten the part.

My other very best friend, Alison, was a drama major, and she and I created some memorable moments all over the city, which we treated as a stage, from going to department stores and pretending we were foreigners speaking gibberish and needing help, to crashing funerals and wakes as "guests" looking for snacks, to displays of faux-fighting on line at the movies. And sometimes we'd park ourselves outside the Plaza Hotel and sing to tourists. I wasn't sure at the time why I was driven to such nutty behavior, but only later did I realize that it's because I longed to be a performer.

Although I graduated from an art school, it never clicked with me that I could be an artist for a career, so when I got to college, I declared my Political Science major the first week. I was either going to be an attorney or go to Wharton School of Business and be a real-life Alex P. Keaton.

I had racked up some college credits in high school, so my first semester was fairly light. I also decided early on that I would take a wide range of classes to fill in the general education requirements for my major, and I had heard that acting class was an easy A, and that all the girls took that class. Look, I was eighteen. I had my priorities. So I enrolled in Acting 101 with Dr. Muriel Kellerhouse for one of my second semester classes.

However, when I showed up for my first class at 9 a.m. at the beginning of second semester, two things happened: 1. There were hardly any hot girls because too many guys had enrolled for the same reason I did, and 2. Something clicked during the first acting exercise, and completely changed the course of my life.

All of us students were crawling on the ground while Dr. Kellerhouse called out scenarios of why we were on the ground. Anything from, "You're under fire in Viet Nam and you're crawling to a fox hole," to, "you're sneaking out of your lover's house while their spouse comes home," and while everyone else seemed to be rolling their eyes and going through the motions, I felt something real, like I was actually there in those moments. My imagination ran wild as I saw and heard explosions and gunfire, or the jealous boyfriend screaming, "Who's here? Where the hell is he," as I crawled to an imaginary window from under the imaginary bed.

In those instances, *I was living other lives.* And I was hooked! I knew I HAD TO DO THIS FOREVER. And so I auditioned for every play in school and went to summer programs in the City every summer to improve my craft. I garnered the leads in most of the shows I did in school, plus I directed and choreographed all the fight scenes and swordplay in the Shakespearean and classical plays (having been a varsity fencer and martial artist throughout high school). I was truly dedicated. I still held my Poli Sci major for a "backup plan," but I knew I was going to act, be in theater, do movies, marry Winona Ryder and live happily ever after in Hollywood.

To be clear, my initial intent in enrolling in that first class was to meet girls. Hey, I was eighteen and I had my priorities. But later, it became about the work. And, truthfully, Winona.

After college, I attended the prestigious New Actors Workshop two-year conservatory program, and had the privilege to be mentored by three legends: Mike Nichols, Paul Sills, and George Morrison. After an article about Mike and his film, *Wolf,* was published in Vanity Fair magazine, in which both he and the journalist briefly praised me and my work in class, a wave of excitement washed over me. There was my name. In Vanity Fair. With Mike Nichols. And Tom Hanks on the cover. My true destiny would be fulfilled. My reality shifted. Here I come, Winona. It's just a matter of time. Now I had street cred.

In 1994 I co-founded the award-wining Off-Broadway theater company, The Greenwich House Theater Company. After one of the performances of the first play we put up, I secured my first manager. From there, I traveled to Los Angeles to meet with the nephew of a family friend, who, at the time, was president of TriStar Pictures (Sony). I also met an agent who signed me the day before I was heading back to New York, so when I got home, I told my parents that I had to move to LA. They were stunned, sad, and excited. My best friend Dave was also excited because all he wanted was for me to meet Tia Carrere and introduce him so they could get married in a double ceremony with me and Winona.

I did mention earlier that my reality had been shifted.

I arrived in LA, called Mike Nichols' agent at CAA, introduced myself over the phone, and said, "I'm here and I'm ready." I had a big set of brass ones, alrighty. That got a chuckle, but I also got the name of three other agents there, whom I met with. They all said they couldn't do anything for me because I was a nobody, but they did task themselves with getting me a local manager, who was big-time... for writers. Still, I was excited that I got a manager, brokered by three power-moguls of the world's most feared talent agencies.

But she managed writers. She didn't know what to do with me. She had connections, so I auditioned for lead roles in pilots and big roles in movies, but I had no credits. All of those roles went to names. So my manager let me go. I was distraught, dejected, broke. Luckily, she did place me at one of the top commercial agencies in town, and let me tell all of you, commercials saved my life. I also had to supplement my sporadic income with steady pay, so I did a lot of temp work, which led to a great job as Production Manager for Backstage West. I was responsible for putting the entire newspaper together with the Art Director, and making them go digital in order to save time and money, but more importantly, so I wouldn't have to be there into the late hours of the night. But it was still a full-time job,and I wanted to have time to audition and act. So sure, was I, of my talent and inevitable success, I left. Fortunately, commercials had picked up at that time.

After years of auditioning for thousands of commercials, and making a great living from residuals, I got burnt out. The bottom line is I had done very little acting in the years I spent pounding the pavement. Plus, I was auditioning so much, I had no time to see friends, leave town, or enjoy Los Angeles. I never really broke into film or television, and upon meeting Winona Ryder (who by, the way, is a lovely human being) at the premiere party for *Alien: Resurrection*, it was clear that we would not be having children together, let alone going on a date. Dave was simultaneously disappointed because I had met Tia Carrere at the same party, but I failed to mention to her that I had found her new husband. Dave didn't talk to me for a week.

In my early years as an actor, I had done a lot of production work and photography (recalling my art background), and although I had no formal business training, I left the industry and utilized my knowledge and talents to go into business for myself. I became a headshot photographer, and quickly rose to the top of the referral lists of many agencies, and then I became a print-casting director for major ad campaigns. But I wanted more experiences and a greater ability to enjoy the life I missed out on while my head was buried in scripts and auditions and workshops.

I'd always been a kind of tech geek, so I went into startups, and worked for some really impressive companies. I learned web design and then I rose to manage designers and other tech positions. I helped launch a multi-million dollar mobile/entertainment company and then became the Director of New Media of a big advertising agency. I also served as a contracted consultant for numerous other businesses helping them run more efficiently, starting and/or fixing departments. I inadvertently had become a successful businessman. And I actually loved it. I'm currently launching a new Internet company and am a founder of Game Nation, a new 10,000 acre theme park opening in Florida in 2018. But I still do photography for fun, and sometimes I direct pet projects. I've done some voice-overs recently because I'm still a performer at heart. Plus, I'm married to the VP of a major agency, so, I'll never be completely out of the business.

However, the day I decided to officially leave acting was simultaneously the saddest and most exhilarating day of my life at that time. I felt I had freed myself from a runaway train, jumping to safety, but being battered and bruised in the process. I loved acting, but I hated the *business*. See, I had been trained as an artist, a craftsman, and had discipline for the craft. But having forgone Wharton School of Business, I knew nothing of *business*, let alone the *business* of acting. And believe me. It is a business. It is an industry. An industry involving everything one may think of by the sheer mention of the word "industry," which includes hundreds of moving parts and positions: labor, manufacturing, carpentry, electricians, engineers, equipment handling, drivers, lighting technicians, textiles and on and on and on and on. And then there are casting directors, writers, producers, directors, studio committees, and on and on and on and on. And then, finally, there are the actors.

And unless one has any kind of business acumen, it is very difficult to understand, as an artist whose sole focus is the craft of self, how we fit into that industry. We are just one small cog in a very, very big wheel.

Although I officially left the business, I am happy and grateful for all the successes I've had, the relationships I've made and kept, and for all the fun I've had, despite the struggles. But because I know first-hand how difficult it can be, especially for actors just starting out, I felt compelled to write this book to dispel any myths, misconceptions, and misinformation.

The industry professionals I've spoken to, although diverse in occupation, background and perspective, touch upon similar ideas which, as you will see, support the notion that there are universal truths to success in this industry.

This book is for you, **The Actor**, pursuing your dreams along a path of uncertainty and fraught with obstacles. I hope to illuminate the process of the *business* so you, as an artist, can have a deeper understanding of how it works, giving you insight as to what goes on "behind the lines" with solid and practical advice from the top people in their field. May you take this information and use it to your advantage and for your success in this business.

Break a leg.

My Life as an Actor
(a.k.a. What *Not* to Do)

My career in the entertainment industry unofficially began when I was in the seventh grade. I say unofficially because I didn't make a conscious decision until many years later, but as fate would have it, at the age of twelve, I was cast in my first role.

Some friends and I cut school at lunchtime to go out to eat. This was not really allowed, but we were rebels. On the way to a store to get some snacks, we were stopped by a guy who asked, "Hey, you kids want to be in a music video?" It was 1982 and MTV was still the biggest thing to have happened to television and music. Only a year on air, and it was pretty much the only channel I watched since day one. "YES," I exclaimed eagerly.

The dude— and I say dude, because he was a total dude, skinny jeans, bandanna, and all— instructed us to go around the corner, walk two blocks, and go down that street where another guy would be waiting for us. My friend Pete was convinced were going to be abducted and was nervous the whole time we walked to where we were told.

When we arrived, there was a guy waiting, who must have been the director, and a few other people including someone holding a large video camera. Sure enough we were about to be in a music video, and we were all so excited. Pete was relieved we weren't about to be kidnapped.

George Thorogood's "Bad to the Bone" was released that year and when the video debuted on MTV, I felt like a movie star because I am clearly featured in the video along with my pals. And thus my career was born.

Years later, my sister called me from a George Thorogood concert to tell me about her surreal moment of watching him on stage with the video playing behind him on a giant screen and seeing me as a little kid.

Back in the mid-90s, I was the lead in an Off-Broadway show called *Acts of Contrition* produced by the award-winning Greenwich House Theater Company, the company I proudly co-founded on Barrow Street in the West Village of New York City. In it, I played a public defender representing someone on death row. To prepare for the role, I walked into New York City's Public Defenders offices and asked if I could come in for a few days and shadow an attorney or two in preparation for the role. They were flattered and granted me access to whomever I wanted. I ended up shadowing the same attorney for a full week while he met with clients, took depositions, went to lunch, and argued in court. The experience was exhilarating because I had never experienced anything like that, and I learned so much, not just about the legal system, but about the mindset and spirit of the attorneys and their clients.

That level of insight can't be learned from reading or hearing about it. And it can't be performed truthfully without first-hand experience.

I had also just graduated a two-year, full-time conservatory program where I worked on my craft tirelessly, so I was in my prime.

As a result, after the final performance of the final weekend, a woman approached me, business card in hand, and the first words out of her mouth were, "Call me tomorrow. I want to manage you." I was speechless.

A moment later, Dan, not knowing that I had gone to school with his cousin, who was also in the play, pushed his way through the crowd and came up to me, business card in hand. All he said was, "I'm a director! Call me!" I was floored.

After a few days, I called Dan and we had a great conversation. He had just graduated School of Visual arts, where instead of making the required short films in the directing program, he directed a low-budget feature film called *Eyes Beyond Seeing*, which was not only excellent, but looked like it was produced for a million dollars. I think it cost less than sixty thousand. Dan was incredibly talented, and he wanted to work with me. He was also moving to Los Angeles later that year and around the same time as I, so we decided to be roommates.

Until that time, the manager who had approached me, Judy, took me on as a client and we worked together for a couple of years, even after I moved to LA. However, the time in New York wasn't fruitful. I would audition quite a bit, but never really booked anything in film or television. I had this amazing training, but I had never taken an audition class. I didn't even know there was such a thing.

After a brief visit to LA where the sole purpose was to meet with a family friend, who just so happened to be president of Tri-Star Pictures, I had signed with my first agent. Judy had placed me with the Coast to Coast Agency, and they signed me across the board.

4

I returned home to let my parents know that I had an agent, and I would be starring in every Tri-Star Pictures film which my soon-to-be roommate, Dan, would direct, so I was moving to Hollywood. I thought, "Damn, I got it made!"

But I didn't. That's not to say I didn't have a lot of fun.

Because Dan and I knew for certain that I would be a movie star and he would be the next Steven Spielberg, we rented what for us was a very expensive apartment with two master suites, two bathrooms, walk-in closets, swimming pool, jacuzzi, barbecue pits and stocked with the latest UCLA co-eds. So sure were we that this place was temporary, until the time we would buy homes right next to each other in the Hollywood Hills, that Dan rented all of the apartment furniture, including his bedroom set, and bought the largest television that could possibly fit in the living room.

I had saved up a lot of money from my day job as a paralegal in my uncle's Park Avenue law firm, and I knew it would only be a matter of minutes before I was not only mentioned in Vanity Fair again, but featured on the cover, so I went out and bought a futon and desk for my bedroom.

And now let me recount the events that led up to all the rental furniture being repossessed.

Upon arriving in LA, I did what every twenty-four year old male on his way to stardom would do: I rented a red convertible Mustang until I could find a car to buy. Dan liked it so much he went out and bought a red convertible Le Baron.

I had taken two part-time jobs to afford what was going to become a very expensive lifestyle. I waited tables at night at a restaurant in Redondo Beach, about forty-five minutes south of LA, and during the day I was an office P.A. for a production company. They didn't last long because I needed to be able to audition, memorize lines, and network.

After Dan and I moved into our apartment, we knew we had to get out there and meet people. Dan's friend and producer of his film, *Eyes Beyond Seeing,* had come to town way ahead of us and had settled into the life of a wannabe producer. Randall had produced an amazing film with Dan, and he also had the good fortune of being related to Jerry Bruckheimer. He was a slick fast talker, flashy, brash— exactly the stereotype of a Hollywood producer, but

5

without the credits or the bankroll. Not that it stopped him from flashing hundred dollar bills at any opportunity.

And this is no slight to Randall. He, in fact, was pretty damn amazing. He could talk his way into anything, any party, any relationship, which is no wonder how he, today, is actually a major player, having produced and/or executive produced over eighty Hollywood films, including some blockbusters. Not only that, but Randall was, and is, also a very generous and gracious person, brashness aside.

With our larger-than-movies attitude, Randall, Dan and I would go hit the Sunset Strip at night to schmooze with other wannabes. We were big-time, and obviously, so was everyone else we met. We all spent money, and a lot of it, every night, four or five or six nights a week. And every one of us knew that in order to be taken seriously, we had to look successful, wealthy, like players.

If you remember the movie *Swingers,* than you got a glimpse of our life— our *night*life! Party to party, club to club. Meeting actresses, models, "producers," "directors," "writers." And let me just say this, everyone in Hollywood was writing the next big screenplay, or so it seemed.

But fun seemed to be all I was having. Auditions were sparse, I wasn't in class because I had to save my money for "networking" at all the latest clubs and going on dates with future starlets, and I was letting my important relationships lapse. Plus, I was living off savings, having quit both jobs for my full-time acting "career."

Randall, no surprise, had befriended Mark Wahlberg, and in turn, so did Dan, and then so did I. Mark had just filmed *Fear* with Reese Witherspoon, which was set to debut soon. He was very focused on being taken seriously as an actor, and he and Dan bonded over film making. While hanging out at the Beverly Hills Hotel, where Mark was living with friends for a bit, they began filming some conversations in the room with Dan's enormous VHS camcorder. The conversations turned into an idea for an improvised short film starring Mark and all his friends, and *16A* was born.

I was lucky enough to be there almost the entire time, helping shoot B-roll on the streets, and also chilling poolside with everyone in a cabana.

Mark is known to have a somewhat troubled past, but I was witness to some of the most hospitable behavior I'd ever seen. It really truly appeared to me that Mark was grateful for all he'd overcome and accomplished in his life, and it showed through his politeness to absolutely everyone, and not just his inner circle. I never expected "Marky Mark" to be kind, generous, or humble. And he absolutely was.

Truth be told, *16A was* never saw the light of day. It was a terrible short film, having had no script and being pieced together from some outrageous nights of partying, but it was extremely fun to make.

Randall, of course, was also tight with Randy Spelling, son of the iconic Aaron Spelling and brother to Tori. I would sometimes accompany Randall to the Spelling mansion in Beverly Hills and sit court-side while he and Randy played tennis.

The mansion was absolutely unbelievable. I remember the first time I was there, thinking, "This closet is the size of my apartment." I had also briefly met Tori in the elevator as we were going up to Randy's room. It was all very surreal, and certainly gave me something to talk about at parties: "Well, I just worked on a film with Mark Wahlberg and while I was at the Spelling mansion, blah blah blah…" All true, but also all b.s. And it counted for nothing in terms of furthering my career.

My friend Stephanie had moved to LA and we started to hang out a bit. One night she called me and told me about a new, swanky bar that had opened on the Strip. Sky Bar was the hottest place to be, and to be seen. So of course, we showed up one night.

There were throngs of people waiting to get in, and no one was going inside unless they were female, hot, and young. Stephanie and I ducked into the hotel to try to enter from the lobby side, and as we were making our way to the velvet rope, someone called my name. I turned around. "Pete?" I was floored.

"Jordan!!" Pete, my best from the third grade, fellow music video star, looking the same, but taller, was standing right in front of me, dressed in black from head to toe. Pete, as it turned out, was the keeper of the velvet rope. From that point on, I was at the top of the guest list any night I wanted to go rub elbows with Hollywood's top posers. Hey, I was one, myself.

Sky Bar. Exclusive. Swanky. Expensive. Super-fun. I met the most interesting people under the stars of this open-air club, by the pool, overlooking the city. I met actual producers and celebrities. I had drinks with Scott Baio, for crying out loud. I was on top of the world. It was surely going to happen for me very soon. After all, I knew "everyone" including Scott Baio!

But I did a lot of waiting for the phone to ring. Sure, I was out meeting people, going to parties in the hills, hob-nobbing, but I wasn't doing any acting.

One day, Dan and I realized we could barely afford this lifestyle. We were shopping at the 99¢ Store for canned food, cereal, milk, eggs, and whatever else we needed. Dan could no longer afford to rent our awesome furniture, so one afternoon, two guys showed up and took it all away. We were left with nothing but a giant TV in an empty room.

For a couple of months, depression set in. We would sit on the floor eating Cheerios using the case to Dan's VHS camcorder as a table, watching this big, stupid television. We rarely checked the mail, but we became awesome chess players. That was about as much as we could do. From time to time, actually, quite often, our upstairs neighbors— two cute girls, of course— would bring us food. Thank God for them.

At one point I was so broke, I went to the Wells Fargo ATM and found I had $1.32 in my account. I thought it would be funny to send that to my buddy Dave in New York as proof that I was "big time," so I printed it out at the ATM. That cost me $1.

Fortunately, I had a full tank of gas so I drove around all day applying at stores like Banana Republic, GAP, Armani Exchange, and Abercrombie for jobs. I was more than desperate considering we were due for another run to the 99¢ Store to stock up on Cheerios, plus the impending rent. And by sheer luck, I got hired that same day at Armani Exchange in Santa Monica. I was going to start in just a couple of days, so I was thrilled.

Judy was still technically my manager, but she was in New York and didn't really have relationships with the casting directors in LA, and I didn't really know how everything worked behind the scenes— in fact, I didn't really know how the business worked at all. I came from New York theater, and I started the theater company. So I lived in a bubble, an insulated little world of what I knew and only what I knew. And in LA, I only knew I was idle, and I hate to be idle. Which is why I was out on the town almost every night of the week.

I mentioned that I had a short-lived day-job as an office P.A. for a VH-1 TV show. While I was still at that job, I would often run into a very nice woman in the elevator who worked two floors below my office. On one occasion, she had mentioned that she was an agent— in fact, she turned out to be *the* Arlene Thornton of Arlene Thornton and Associates, one of the most reputable voiceover and commercial agencies in town, as I later found out. Upon hearing that, I let her know that I was an actor currently represented elsewhere but I was not going out on auditions, so I wanted a change in representation. What I failed to mention was that I was doing absolute zero to further my career.

Arlene ended up representing me for just over a year. When I made the switch, my previous agent was furious. And she had the absolute right to be. After all, it had only been less than a year, no casting directors in town knew me, and all I had was theater credits. Plus, I did nothing except to call every week and annoy them with idiotic questions, like, "Why is it so slow," or, "How come I'm not auditioning?" The few times I did audition, I never got a callback.

It wasn't until a year later after I had been dropped by Arlene's agency that I had my first inkling about how the industry worked, and that I couldn't just sit around. So I began to take matters in to my own hands, which dramatically improved my career and my life.

I had the good fortune to have been under the tutelage of the iconic Mike Nichols, Academy Award-winning director and the other half of the legendary comedy duo Nichols & May. And Mike liked me. A lot. And because of that, I was able to get a meeting at Creative Artists Agency, CAA, the most feared agency in the world at that time. I say feared because back in the early '90s, Mike Ovitz wielded a power unlike any other agent. He was a star-make and a ball-breaker. Fortunately, my meeting was not with him.

I met with three agents, all of whom were very powerful, very connected, and very kind. Because I wasn't a movie star, they wouldn't officially represent me, but they did like me, and I had this amazing personal referral from one of the greatest directors in history, who was repped by CAA. So they helped out a little. They helped place me with a new manager, Linn, who in turn got me a new commercial agent. She also was able to send me on pilot auditions. During this period, Dan would always get wide-eyed every time a script would be delivered to me at the apartment with a solid red cover and big, white letters spanning the cover that read "CAA." I felt like I was on top of the world. I had a great manager who got me auditions, a new commercial agent, scripts coming to the door, a job. Things were really beginning to turn around. I always felt bad that I had left Judy, who was the first person other than my folks or my friends to believe in me and my career. But she understood that she couldn't do much being in New York.

While on a roll, I figured I could reach out to someone who said he would meet with me when I moved to LA. After a year had gone by, it was time to reach out to see what might happen.

Years before, Bill Pullman, star of *Ruthless People, Independence Day,* and *Space Balls* was the keynote speaker at my college graduation, and after the ceremony, he was hanging out with us seniors at the afterparty. He was a totally cool cat. I told him I was going to be an actor, and he said, "Well, look me up if you ever come to LA."

After sending a heartfelt letter to his business manager, he invited me to his office, which was in the same building as my commercial agency, Special Artists Agency, one of the top in the industry. I would occasionally be invited back to hang out at his office, "Big Town Productions," but I never asked for any favors. So none were given. I eventually fell out of touch with Bill because I felt like I had nothing to offer, and I didn't want to ask him for help, although I'm sure he would have helped if asked.

After my first pilot season with Linn— a season where I was reading for lead roles against people like Fred Savage and Johnny Galecki, both of whom had a massive list of credits from the time they were children— and not booking a single thing, Linn dropped me. I was devastated. At least I still had a job and a girlfriend.

I had met Julie several months earlier at a theater company we were both part of and we started dating almost immediately, much to the chagrin of the company's founder, who was in love with her. So my time in the company was short-lived.

There were great people in the company, one of whom was Brynn Hartman, Phil Hartman's wife. In fact, Phil and I had become close for a short period of time before his and Brynn's tragic, untimely demise. I had written *Tree Tings,* a short comedic film about a young kid (me) who needed a job and was hired by a mob boss (Phil) to do "tree tings" for him over the course of one day. After Phil's murder, I couldn't bring myself to ever do the film since I'd written the part specifically for him.

After I left the theater company, Julie and I continued

seeing each other. My manager had dropped me at this point, and although I was with a great commercial agency, I wasn't auditioning a lot. I was a bit depressed, and a bit broke. The job at Armani Exchange at least enabled me to scrape by for a while. But it had other benefits that I never saw coming. I got to meet great people. One day Bernadette Peters and her husband, Micheal came into the store. I helped them pick out some tee shirts, and we had a lovely conversation. I was sad to hear that he had passed away a few years ago.

One day while folding jeans to hang on the racks, a short, but very tough-looking guy interrupted my task with a polite, "Pardon me." I turned around and immediately my eyes widened. "Oh my God," I exclaimed. "Ray 'Boom Boom' Mancini!"

He humbly smiled, a bit embarrassed, but happy that I knew who he was. How could I not? He was one of the greatest Lightweight boxers ever, and, not that I was such a huge boxing fan, but I grew up watching him. And he was such a sweet guy. We talked for over half an hour as he told me about his new career as an actor, and I told him about my fledgling career as one. We bonded instantly and kept in touch, having an occasional lunch at his favorite place, the Spitfire Grill near the small-ish Santa Monica Airport. Ray was also producing and starring in a remake of *Body and Soul*. The original starred John Garfield and is considered one of the greatest boxing films of all time.

Ray and I had become good friends and he gave me a small part in the film. I was so thrilled because my career was stagnant. And boy, did I get the royal treatment— first class flight to Reno, where we shot it, hotel, meals, per diem. Plus I got to meet Jennifer Beals, Ray Montegna, and Michael Chiklis, all of whom were in it. My scene was at the end of the film in which I play a hotel valet taking Ray's car for him. All my lines got cut, but I remain credited. To this day I get the occasional residual check for $1.42, or thereabout.

Ray and I stayed in touch for a while, but as I sunk into a deeper depression, that relationship lapsed, as well. I supplemented my career by going to parties with Julie, and I was still extroverted when I could motivate.

One night, Dan, Julie and I were lazing around on our sofas, donated by our neighbors because we couldn't afford to buy any furniture, watching the Oscars on our enormous TV. After the

Oscars ended, news coverage of all the afterparties began, and one reporter, who was on camera, said, "I'm standing here in front of Maple Drive for what is surely the party of the night! Elton John's fiftieth birthday/Oscar Celebration."

Maple Drive? MAPLE DRIVE? That's where my commercial agent's office is! That's also where Bill Pullman's office is! I KNOW that building! I turned to Julie and announced, "We are going to that party!"

She and Dan looked at me like I was crazy. We were sitting around in our sweats, unshowered, and uninvited. "What? No we're not. You're not serious," she insisted. But I was more than serious.

"I own a tux, you're a freaking model and have nice dresses, we're going! " And that was that. We showered quickly, and I changed into my tux. We then drove from West LA to Sherman Oaks so she could put on a gown and grab her makeup, which she would apply during the car ride back to Beverly Hills.

As we approached the neighborhood where the party was in my little white Volkswagen Jetta (not conspicuous at all, right?) Julie started to get nervous. Everyone was arriving in limos, there were police everywhere, and many streets were blocked off so there was no direct route unless you were in a limo. Fortunately, I knew the neighborhood and proceeded to drive down the alleys, unnoticed. We came out behind the barricades near the parking garage of 345 Maple Drive, which to our luck, was open. So I drove into the garage and parked. Julie, shocked, turned to see my ear-to-ear grin.

We made our way to the elevator, got in and pressed the button to the main floor. As we ascended, we could hear the commotion inside the building. The elevator doors opened. There were throngs of people in the lobby, the party was in full swing. As we stepped out of the elevator, a giant, burly bouncer in a tuxedo stopped us.

"Wrist bands." Julie and I looked at each other, confused. "Wrist bands, please," he demanded again. And in that instant, I became possessed. This guy was at least twice my size and I got in his face, screaming at him in Italian, while Julie just glared at him. I was relentless, backing him up, slinging vicious insults at him in a language he couldn't comprehend. Obviously we were supposed to be there, and he had the gall to question that? He finally gave up and let us pass.

Julie was gripping my hand and could barely contain herself. WE WERE IN! And more unbelievable... I don't speak a lick of Italian. Not a single word. It was all gibberish.

That night, we met Sting, and Elton, and Lionel Ritchie. In fact, he and I struck up a conversation while he was making his way to what seemed to be a VIP section. I had noticed that he was wearing two wristbands, and as we got to the door of this other exclusive area, the guy at the door just assumed that since we were walking and talking to Lionel Ritchie, that we must be with him. So he let us in.

We then proceeded to sit at a dinner table with Mr. Ritchie, and following us were Joel and Ethan Coen, Frances McDormand, Bill Macy, Felicity Huffman, and they all sat at our table. The Coen Brothers and Ms. McDormand had just won Oscars for *Fargo*, which they placed on the table. Julie and I introduced ourselves, and we all had dinner together. At one point, I said to Joel Coen about the golden statue before him, "That looks heavy." He smiled and responded, "It is. See for yourself," and he handed it to me. Statue in hand, I was speechless. "You can't take it home, it's mine," he joked, and I handed it back immediately. And you know what? It was heavy.

Days later, I was still on a high from that experience, and it lifted me out of my depression. It even made me a bit more motivated. I quit the job at the Armani Exchange and started doing headshots. After all, I had been a photographer since I was seventeen, and turned pro when I was twenty. I also got a job working in casting. It was more flexible, and it was closer to acting. I learned a great deal from (the now late) Melissa Martin, whom I assisted for a brief period. And then it happened. I had booked my first big commercial. An American Express spot with Jerry Seinfeld. And then a national car spot, and then I was on a roll.

It all changed when it was suggested by my agents to take a commercial workshop with Stuart K. Robinson, regarded as the top commercial audition coach. And it made all the difference in the world. I went from no action, to booking in a matter of weeks after I had finished the workshop.

Over the years, I had auditioned for thousands of commercials, booking only a small, but very highly paid percentage. But for most of them, I was called back and on "avail," short for available, and meaning it was down to me and maybe one or two other people. I never really broke into film and TV like I wanted, but I also didn't do a whole lot except wait for the phone to ring.

One year, I decided to go to Sundance to network, although I had no film there. I just wanted to go, so a few friends and I organized a trip in 1999. Once there, I really had a blast. Not only did I crash every big party, but I got ten or more of my friends in, as well. I was the party crasher king.

My friend Lisa, who founded Acme Talent and Literary Agency, was at Sundance that year, and I recall standing inside the Miramax party, which was *the* party to attend (and one I was certainly not on the list for), talking to the Sundance-winning director, Tony Bui, and looking outside to see Lisa trying to get in. I walked over to the guy in charge of the list, pointed to Lisa and said, "It's okay, she's with me." He immediately let her in from the cold. What's funny is Lisa was actually invited. I had also gotten several friends into a party at a local bar to see Cheryl Crow perform that I did not go to myself. And during that whole experience, I met a ton of people who all came to a post-Sundance party I co-hosted with Lisa and Acme. Despite knowing so many people, it never got me anywhere.

After years of grinding away, auditioning commercially three or four times a day, sometimes five or six days a week, I got burnt out. Mostly, because living in LA, the driving got to me. Going from West Hollywood (where I lived at the time with my first wife) to Burbank to Santa Monica to Hollywood really made me miserable. I spent most of my life in my car and I surely had more to contribute to the planet than exhaust pollution.

By the time I really understood the entertainment business and how it worked, I had no desire to be in it as an actor any more. So I quit. I went on to direct some things, I started my own casting company for print campaigns, and I went back to photography.

I then worked in startups and held a director position at an ad agency. I gladly had moved on from acting, or rather, the pursuit of acting. And I say that because I did very little acting over the course of that ten-year period. It was mostly driving and auditioning. Plus acting in commercials was not, to me, really acting because there was nothing to sink my teeth into— not like creating a character in the theater. All my training, my love of the craft, was gone.

Having been on the other side of the camera or desk as a

director, casting director and ad agency creative, I saw everything about the industry I never was able to see while I was immersed in it, and I have since been helping others understand it much sooner than I ever did.

I did everything one *should not* do: I sat and waited for the phone to ring day after day after day, I waited for the phone to ring some more, I took two audition classes in that entire ten-year span, and not for very long, I relied on meeting people at clubs and parties, I crashed parties, and I relied too heavily on my agents and managers to make my career for me. I had a lot of fun and met a ton of amazing people along the way, but never really treated my career as a business.

Looking back, and I know it's cliché, had I known then what I know now, maybe things would have gone differently. But maybe not. Remember, my initial impulse to act was to meet girls in college. And although I loved the theater and working on the craft, my reason for staying in the business was to make money. And my pursuit of that got me farther away from being an artist and loving the process like I used to in my early days. So I had started out for the wrong reasons, and pursued it in LA from the wrong perspective.

So what should one do in order to really be successful as an actor?

First, you must realize that agents and managers are part of your team, but you have to be the captain of the team. You must be in class, always, you must produce your own work, you must create and maintain and nurture your relationships with people. To rely on others to do all of that for you is like waiting for the Titanic to go around the iceberg. You may know all of this already, which puts you a lot farther ahead of where I was years ago, but it always helps to hear it again, and from someone else.

Often, I'll meet an actor who doesn't understand why they should have both a manager and an agent. "Why should I pay ten percent to an agent and then another ten or fifteen percent to a manager, too?" A valid question I've heard over and over again, but to that I say, because anyone who takes an interest in you and can help further your career, you want them on your team! When you become big and famous, you can choose what you want to do, but believe me, the more people you have working on your behalf, the better. Especially if you're just starting out.

Plus, as you read the interviews, you'll understand the significant difference between agents and managers. They do very different things, and although there may be crossover, they each handle aspects of your career differently. Two heads, or more, are always better than one.

And if you are fortunate enough to obtain any kind of representation, you must work ten times as hard than when you were on your own. I know it sounds odd that once you have someone handling your career that you have to personally work even harder, but it's true. You have to have things— work— for them to promote. Remember, you're not going to be the only client someone represents, nor are you necessarily going to be at the top of their list. Sure they may believe in you, but agents and managers believe in all their clients. They must handle everyone, and the ones that book more are the ones they spend more attention on because they are easier to sell.

This is a business, and as an actor, you are a commodity. So you must work especially hard to rise to the top, even when you have someone, or a group of people, on your team. Being successful is a team effort. No single person can do it alone. Not an actor, an agent, a manager, attorney… No one. And that's actually true for any business. It takes a team to build a company, a product, a service. It certainly takes a team to build a career, and you must be the team captain.

But don't just take my word for it. Read what the experts have to say.

Good luck on your journey.

The Reps

Brianna Ancel
Vice-President, Clear Talent Group

You may notice that Brianna and I share the same last name. That's because I have the good fortune to be married to her, which makes for an easy interview.

Brianna began her career in the dance department at the Kazarian/Spencer Agency as an assistant to Tim O'Brien. She, herself, had been a dancer since childhood, having earned a Bachelor of Fine Arts degree for Choreography from U.C. Irvine. Her extensive experience in dance helped her move into the role of Assistant Director of KSA's dance department in 2000, where she remained for a couple of years.

Then, in 2003, Tim decided it was time to leave KSA, and started Clear Talent Group, bringing Brianna with him. Although her background was in dance, Brianna always had a passion for all aspects of the arts, and began the theatrical department upon the new agency's doors opening for business.

Over the last ten years, she has grown the department, and the agency, representing actors who've appeared on most major network and cable series, and in countless films. As Vice President, she's had the honor of being nominated for the Talent Manager Association's *Seymour Heller Award* for best Adult Theatrical Agent of The Year for the past three consecutive years.

Because of our relationship, I witness— first-hand and on a daily basis how hard she works for her clients, how much of herself she gives to their success and her position at the agency— that it is no wonder to me that she's been nominated three years in a row by her peers. For that (and because she's my wife), I thought she would make a great first interview for the book. And as the first interviewee, I've asked her to take us through her entire process, and to start with the basics.

Me: Brianna, could you please explain the difference between what an agent does and what a manager does?

Brianna:	This is a question I get a lot. The primary answer to that is an agent handles the business side of an actor's career and a manager tends to, well, they are still concerned with business but they also put a lot of attention on their clients' personal path for their career, and every aspect of their career— whether that be their film career as an actor, as a writer, as a director, all facets of their career— whereas an agent may be specified in one particular field. Managers also tend to have fewer clients whereas agents have a larger list of clients.
Me:	How is the business different today than say, five or ten years ago?
Brianna:	With television, there are a lot more scripted shows out there. Cable networks are writing more and more content. With reality TV being so popular, there was a time period where scripted television was really hurting. But cable networks and new media outlets like Hulu and YouTube and Netflix and Amazon are now all creating original content. The sky is the limit with the Internet as an outlet for broadcasting content. It's exciting, but it's very vast, and it's hard to pick and choose the best among it all.
	Also, there has been a tremendous amount of production that's called "runaway production" that takes work out of Los Angeles, so that there's fewer work opportunities for local actors and it becomes more competitive. Plus, there's been more crossover between the film actor and the television actor, whereas before, there might have been a very clear distinction about the genre that an actor primarily works in. Especially with celebrities and stars now, that's more of a gray area. You have a lot of film stars doing television and even vice versa. People bounce back and forth.
Me:	How does that affect the competition then in terms

of people who are not names? Is it more difficult for them to obtain any kind of role on TV, whether it's a small under-five, or what they used to call a day-player role, or a guest star? Also, does it then create a bigger difficulty for TV actors getting roles in films— even smaller roles in films— if they are just starting out? Or even known actors as well?

Brianna: Yeah, everybody wants to work and so it does create a more competitive field.

Me: Even though there are more outlets available, it's still more competitive?

Brianna: Well, yes, because not everything is shooting here in LA or in New York, and so it just gets more spread out. With more outlets it also means it requires more money to be spread out amongst everything, so budgets aren't the same as they used to be. It used to be that independent film was a really good place for a new up-and-coming actor to get noticed with a great film lead. Now those projects are so contingent on attaching big names to get funding because it's their only way to get a good budget, making those opportunities slimmer.

The TV roles where you used to book a guest star— and once you reach that level, that would be where you were at— you could book those consistently. But it's just so much more competitive with these bigger names who are more willing to do those roles. I feel like it's important to not pay attention so much to the billing, or even the size of the role, or how many days you're working, but what is the nature of the role, and is it significant, and does it have meaning for you, and is it going to beget further work with that producer or that director or some other people on the project.

It's not uncommon for an actor to have a small part, they get on set and everybody loves what they do and the writers write that part further. It's all in what you make of it.

Me: With it being so competitive, even though there's more outlets available, what do you think actors should do to be more proactive and productive with their career instead of that old stereotype of sitting around waiting for the phone to ring?

Brianna: I think more than ever, actors need to be more proactive. Try to be as multi-faceted as you can, meaning write stuff, collaborate with people, shoot things you can post online, start to create your own hype using the Internet and social media and get yourself noticed in that way if you're not getting noticed through the more traditional outlets of having an agent or manager submit you, or if you don't have an agent or a manager.

It's a great time for actors to take their career into their own hands because of how the Internet has made it so easy to self-market yourself. Without your own website and being active on social media, you're really missing an opportunity to create a fan base. Rather than relying on somebody else to discover you, you can make yourself known.

Me: Do you think then, in your opinion, that actors need to be better business people, because the idea is that, "We're artists, that's our thing, we're not good business people, which is why we need an agent or manager or some type of team?" But if you don't have that already, what do you think their emphasis on actual business should be once they have the craft down or at least they're studying?

Brianna: You have to look at it like a business because what else is it? It's your artistry and it's your craft but anytime you want to make a living from something or you want to make money from something, it automatically

22

becomes a business and you can't just rely on an agent or a manager to be the only one that looks at your work career as a business. You're missing an opportunity to have more things happen.

When you're able to marry your business mind with your artist mind, you're going to have much more success because you'll be able to better organize and see paths and apply things— like marketing and financial organization— and you'll be able to survive better. You won't just be a starving artist. When you can apply more of a business mind to what you are doing, your career will end up paying off in the long run.

Me: In terms of the business aspect of acting, what kinds of specific things can you recommend that actors do to either learn the business of acting in the entertainment industry or further their knowledge and success in the business?

Brianna: You have to read my book, *Ten Top Tens From a Ten Percenter*, in which one of those categories is "Ten ways to treat your career as a business."

Me: Can you give us maybe one or two of those ways? Just to give people a little taste of the kinds of things that it takes?

Brianna: Absolutely. One very simple thing that should be obvious to any other business person— but it's not always obvious to actors— is to have a business card for yourself. People carry around headshots and resumes— and not even that much these days because everything is digital— but you never know who you're going to run into. Especially in Los Angeles or New York when every fifth person you bump into is in the industry.

As you network and you have conversations, don't

23

rely on just, "Let me get your information and I'll call you." Be able to give them something to remember you by. That's a little thing that can make a big impact and it's relatively inexpensive.

Me: Do you recommend the kind with the actor's photo on it or a straight business card?

Brianna: I think a photo card can be great because it will make them remember you because if they look at your name and they're just like, "Who was that guy?" If you're able to write something on that business card on the back, like, "We met at such and such," that'll ring some bells. And do your best to get someone's information as well. Not everyone is forthcoming with it, depending on whom you're talking to, but if you can get that exchange, it'll put some control in your hands to do some follow-up.

Me: In terms of establishing relationships, which is what we're talking about, they say, in the industry, it's all about who you know. Obviously there needs to be some talent and there needs to be some business savvy, but how much of it depends on relationships, and what are one or two things that people can do to nurture those relationships without portraying the "needy actor" type?

Brianna: Relationships are huge. When you think about it, this business is different because any given job or project usually lasts for a short period of time, as opposed to someone who works at a company for years and years and years. When you're moving from job to job, and other people move from job to job, the more people you can stay in contact with as they move around, you want to move around with them.

Meaning, if you have an opportunity to work with people on a film, that director is going to be onto something next; that producer is going to be

24

onto something next; that DP is going to be onto something next; that show-runner is going to be onto something next. So it's this web of contacts that you want to stay in touch with because everybody is going to be moving on and you want to stay within that club of people that you've worked with because you can then follow them if they want to work with you.

Stay in contact and let people know what you're doing, even if it's a quick email or postcard now and then to check in. You certainly don't want to ask questions like, "What are you working on? Is there a part for me?" You can be a little more subtle than that. Approach it from a place where you're truly interested in what's going on with them because you truly care about their career and then you know, have your career be secondary when you're reaching out to people. That will prevent [the perception] of that neediness that you're talking about.

Me: Basically you're saying take a genuine interest in others.

Brianna: Yes. If you take a genuine interest in what they are doing then you're going to be able to nurture those relationships more and more, and it'll turn into more of a friendship. They'll want to help you, you'll want to help them, as opposed to being more one-sided and that you just want something from them. It's also important to share all of your relationships with your agent or manager.

             We can't know everybody in this business and we can't know everybody our clients know in this business, so we need to be reminded and be told about people you meet because we can always try to capitalize on those relationships and do some of that follow up and nurturing of relationship for you.

Me: You talk a lot about following people from job to job, like directors or producers and obviously that happens with agents and casting directors, too, because they frequently move from company to company. But what if you're just a newcomer and you don't have that opportunity, or haven't yet had the opportunity to work with people? What's the best way to begin a relationship and nurture it from a genuine perspective even though we all know that there is an agenda?

Brianna: I think it's the same. You may not meet those people from working with them so you've got to ask yourself, where am I going to meet these people? You can do that through networking events, there are showcases that you can be involved in... if you hear about screenings of projects, or if you have a friend that's involved with something, that's an opportunity for you to be in a place where there's other industry people.

You may have to put in a little more work, but honestly, even the working actor needs to be thinking about these things, too, because once you start to get complacent about keeping your networking up, you'll start to feel the side effects of that. If you don't have an agent or manager, and only have a smaller resume of work, you're just going to have to look for those opportunities a little bit more. You can start small. There are student films and grad films and AFI projects— those are all people starting out, too.

One of the best things to do is if you can create those relationships when you're starting out and a director is starting out, or a producer is starting out— or even a casting director who was an associate and she or he is casting a small project for the first time— you're all at the same level where you're building your careers. If you can stick it out with those people, they'll remember you. You were all there for each other when your careers were in their infancy. There's plenty of celebrities and stars out there… why does Todd Phillips always hire the same actors? Well, because all along, these were people that he loved to work with, they helped each other out at some point when they weren't household names. Same goes for a lot of circles of actors and directors.

Me: Then, what would be some really great tip or advice you could give to someone who is just coming out of an acting program that hasn't had the experience, or doesn't' even necessarily know where to begin? I don't want to give away anything from your forthcoming book, but what are one or two things that the absolute newcomer <u>must do or must know or must learn</u>?

Brianna: Well, you've got to be willing to work for free initially, or for very little money. I think that's just the name of the game. And know that it won't always be that way, but it's a good place to start to build some of those relationships and get a resume. You've got to surround yourself with people who are like-minded and in the industry. I think it's wonderful and essential for every actor to have a life outside of the industry, just to take a break because it can get crazy, but I think it's also important to have a support group not only to help keep you sane when you feel like you want to give up, but to also collaborate with, talk to, and see what other people are doing.

You just have to put yourself out there. Have a presence with the casting sites online and some of the acting communities that are out there online. It'll help you feel like you're not alone and it'll definitely give you some ideas of ways you might be able to be proactive when you're feeling like a small fish in a very big pond.

Me: How often do you take clients with little or no credits, if ever?

Brianna:	I have to be really wowed by their talent and be able to see a spark of potential there, and usually if I'm going to do that, it's going to be an actor that's on the younger side. It's a little bit harder with actors that are say, forty and over, because most of the working actors in that demographic have large resumes and it's very competitive. And personally, I've just found that's an area where I've just seen a lot of challenges. For a younger actor, it makes more sense that you're not going to have a big resume and if I can really see that there's that "it" factor, then I'll take the time to bring somebody on to develop them.
	Sometimes I recommend that before getting with an agent in that scenario is to get with a manager who can really help groom you and get you ready to be with an agent. That is one mistake I think people make: they either go to acting school and they graduate or they take some classes for a couple of years, or even less than that, and they assume that they're ready for it all. "I'm ready for an agent, I'm ready for a manager, I'm ready to audition for the big stuff," but that's not always the case. I've seen it happen where an actor hasn't gone through enough training and their audition technique isn't great, and they're not ready to make that impression in the room, and then they blow it. The casting people remember that, and they don't get called back into that room for a long time. You're much better off putting in the legwork, the training and the education, and then saying, "Okay, now I'm really ready."
Me:	What can hold an actor back from getting work in this industry or furthering a relationship within this industry?
Brianna:	Well, the obvious ones: don't be a jerky, needy, prima donna actor. On every film or TV show, there are hundreds of people that are necessary in order for that show to be successful, and the actors are just one

component. The amount of pre-production that goes into a film before they even start shooting the actors is tremendous. For the actor, because they're the one that's on camera, they're the one that is the household name, that the public is going to know about, I think it's really easy to forget that they are just one of many, many people that make a project possible.

If you start to get too much of an ego about that and it shows, well, people aren't going to want to work with you because what you're saying is that, "I'm more important than you are," and you have some sense of entitlement. You just have to treat everybody nicely. It goes back to nurturing those relationships, and you want to work with those people on their next project, so it doesn't serve you or the project to bring any kind of attitude that says, "I'm better than you." That's a huge mistake that actors can make. Be somebody that people would want to work with again.

Me: What is your biggest challenge as an agent— and not just an agent, but the vice president of an agency? What does your typical day look like?

Brianna: As an agent for film and television, I'm constantly submitting on projects all day long but that's the bare minimum. In this business I have to go above and beyond, and that means putting in the calls and the pitches, trying to get people in the door and convince others that they should see somebody. In some ways, my challenges aren't different from an actor's challenges. Actors want "the yes." Everybody wants somebody to say yes. Oftentimes, a lot of yeses have to happen before it actually gets to the actor. I'm only one of those.

I'm one of the people that needs to say yes to the actor, and there's people that need to say yes to me. Then there's people that need to say yes to those people and so on! A lot of cooks in the kitchen, and for me, the challenge is often convincing all of those people either one at a time or collectively— however it might happen— that out of all of these hundreds of actors, I have got somebody that they don't know that's worth seeing. That's where *my* relationships and the trust that *I've* built with people comes into play. Without that, my chances of somebody listening, especially if they don't know the actor, is going to be even harder.

As a vice-president of an agency, I have to pay attention to the overall image of the company and where we want to grow, and make sure that how I go about representing my people is consistent with that message and what we are known for— which is a lot of personal service to our clients, and being progressive and forward thinkers, and agents that are really great to work with both from a client's point of view and a buyer point of view.

Me: Which is why you've been nominated three years in a row for Best Adult Theatrical Agent of the Year and by adult, I don't mean porn.

Brianna: That's right! I like to think that those nominations come from the combination of everything I spoke about and I'm very proud of that.

Me: What do you love about your job?

Brianna: Well... It depends on the day. I love telling someone they booked a job, I love helping somebody achieve their dreams and knowing that I played a part in it. Helping them create a new relationship— one that they couldn't have done on their own, or they didn't think that they could on their own— facilitating those opportunities, building something together. And I like being part of a team in that regard, and when the team works really well, it's even more exciting.

Me:	What do you love about actors? And not just the ones you represent but in general?
Brianna:	They are entertaining. They entertain me. I love television, I love film. These are people that can take us to another place. A talented actor is an amazing entertainer for what they are able to… for how they are able to transport us for a couple of hours, or whatever that might be, and that's not an easy thing to do. I think for what they provide to society— that entertainment value and that escapism— I love actors for that. I also respect actors tremendously because this career is not easy at all.
	What I admire are the ones that stick with it and have tremendous passion about what they do. To have found something that you have that kind of passion for and stick with— I really respect. When I see that in an actor, that's what makes me want to work hard for somebody.
Me:	I think that a lot of actors have an idea that once they have an agent, everything is taken care of, or a manager but there's a lot that goes on behind the scenes that many people don't really know or understand because often one may hear a complaint of, "Oh, my agent never sends me out," but can you dispel that myth that it's not the, "lazy agent" that there's so much more being done on the actor's behalf that they just don't know about and whether they go out or not has nothing to do with the agent.
Brianna:	Yeah, I think it would be of tremendous value for any actor to sit in an agent's chair for a couple of days to understand what it's all about. I think actors need to realize that they're not the only client. That means that it's not about them every hour of the day. I have to balance my time as best as possible among all my clients. I think that every agent or manager would love to just have one single client they could work

for the entire time. It would make for a beautiful relationship, but that's just not realistic. So for an actor to realize that and then also know that we want all of our clients to go out as often as possible.

Every actor wants to be auditioning more, that never changes. Even if you audition five times a week, it still could be more. They just want as many opportunities as possible, and I get that, and I wish the same for my clients, and I'm sure every agent does. We're not intentionally wanting to hold you back. My goal is always to try and get my actors out as much as possible but it is a matter of balancing time and it's matter of breaking down those walls in casting offices that aren't familiar with somebody. It's sometimes just a total lottery based on the hundreds of actors being submitted for one role and who is going to get called in and—

Me: Sometimes thousands of submissions?

Brianna: Often thousands! It can definitely be a lottery. To say that an agent has the sole control of whether or not you're getting that audition is a *really naïve way of thinking* because of all of these other factors that are involved. While I think the smart actors understand that, I think it's still one of the hardest things about this business that any actor has to just trust and realize: "Okay, I know my agent wants me to be working and they're doing what they can even if it doesn't feel like it." They don't see everything that goes on behind the scenes: the phone calls or the emails or the submissions, or whatever it might be.

Me: What is your biggest pet peeve?

Brianna: I think probably... well, maybe two things. One is poor communication of the basic stuff, like availability and other jobs they have, or even like, "I met somebody important," and they never told me about it— a director or casting director, or somebody— or even a small audition that they got from their own submission on an independent project and I didn't hear about it. In my opinion, if it has to do with your acting career, I should be in the loop about it. And also things like how you're feeling about a particular audition, or are we on the right track?

I've had actors come to me and say, "You know, I just feel like I haven't been going out on the right stuff." Well, if you've been feeling that way, why haven't we talked about it sooner? Do you feel like these roles that I'm targeting for you aren't right? Are your pictures saying something different?

Communication to me is a *really huge thing,* so if it's lacking, or someone is really aloof or distant, it's a big deal. If they're also not getting results or I'm not getting results, it can be one of my biggest factors in discontinuing to represent somebody.

Me: You mentioned the actor's pictures being representative of what you are going for. What do you look for in a headshot for people who are submitting to you for the first time and also what do you look for from your clients?

Brianna: For new actors or new potential clients— depending on whether they had representation before or not?

Me: Assuming not.

Brianna: Assuming not, okay. I would say I don't necessarily expect them to have the most amazing, professional picture. In fact, in some ways, if they've spent hundreds of dollars on a photo shoot before getting with an agent, there can be some disappointment because it could be that none of those pictures will work and they have to re-shoot. In my opinion, one strong shot that represents who they are— that's enough for me.

Then we talk about going into another photo shoot.
I do film and television and so I'm not a huge fan of
having ten different looks. Commercial agents, I find,
prefer that because that's just a different world and
there's a different casting process involved— it's much
quicker, it's more character based— so those kinds
of pictures work better. But in film and television, I
generally think you can get by with three, maybe four
pictures that really represent an actor's niche, and you
work with your agent or manager on that to make
sure you get what you need.

Me: Can you tell me an inspiring or Cinderella-type story?

Brianna: One of my favorite stories is a client who I pitched for
            what was to be a small-ish single-episode role on the
            Showtime series, *Weeds*. He got the part and we found
            out that once he shot the first episode, his role was
            probably going to reoccur in at least one more episode.
            And then I was starting to get good feedback. They
            were loving him on set! The first season, he ended
            up in seven episodes, and then after that he went on
            to work three seasons as a reoccurring guest star on
            the show, and I think in total, he worked about 20
            episodes over three seasons.

            I love that story because, as I mentioned earlier, you're
            not always at the mercy of the writers. You can
            sometimes go in and convince people that you are an
            interesting actor, and what you are bringing to the
            character is fun and interesting to the project. And if
            you can convince them of that, they'll say, "We want
            this person in the show."

Me: Plus you said they loved him on set. So also be likable
            and be someone that people want to work with.

Brianna: Exactly! It's a combination of your talent and your choices as an actor, and what you bring to the role, and also being a professional and someone people love to work with.

* * *

Brianna's book, **Ten Top Tens From a Ten Percenter**, *is an all-encompassing career guide from Agent to Actor, and will be available Fall of 2013.*

David Ziff,
Senior Vice-President, CESD

Cunningham, Escott, Slevin & Doherty was originally founded in the mid-1960s by Bill Cunningham with TJ Escott establishing the New York office in 1971. Then, in 2005, Ken Slevin and Paul Dougherty added their names to this prestigious moniker.

David Ziff is not only the Senior Vice-President of this globally respected talent agency, he heads the commercial talent division, which is considered one of the best in the world. I've had the privilege of knowing David casually for a few years, and he's a truly great guy. Direct, blunt, dry-humored, he embodies everything a great agent should, including a great eye for talent.

Me: Hey David.

David: Hey buddy.

Me: Hey, thank you so much for taking the time to do this. I know…

David: Yeah, yeah, yeah, yeah whatever. (Laughter)

Me: Alright, so let's get right into it.

David: Alright, brother. Go ahead, shoot.

Me: What strategies do you practice when representing a newcomer, if you represent newcomers? And do you represent newcomers?

David: Sure. We don't look to add-on to our client list. We look to fill in little areas that we're missing.

           We tell the client to send out postcards. We give them labels with all the casting directors we use and they put together a post card, and then they send it to all the casting directors saying, "I'm now with CESD."

We'll also let the casting directors know that we now represent so and so. We'll send their reel over if the person is not known.

We're pretty proactive. We usually ask newcomers and new people to get new pictures because we like to start fresh. And that's important. Pictures are everything for [online] casting services like LA Casting and Casting Frontier.

Me: What do you want in headshots? What do you want the actors to try and convey in headshots when you're sending them to get new photos taken?

David: It depends on what type of role it is but usually the word I like to throw out there is "approachable." We don't want anyone to be turned off looking at the pictures.

For our character guys we want everything from the couch potato or the gas station attendant all the way up to the lawyer in a courtroom— and everything in between— then we'll have them go in unshaven and scruffy and messy with a t-shirt, and then we'll have them bring in a white shirt and a nice tie and be clean-shaven with their hair a bit to the side— and everything in between, like a dad with a sweater on or a blazer, a pair of jeans— whatever it is.

Your picture is your first audition and they're becoming more and more important. The casting directors say we have good pictures. We have great photographers we use. One in particular is doing a great job because he's changing with the times. We had a couple of photographers that were on our list that just didn't get it after a while. The colors have to be brighter these days. They have to pop off the screen and the one guy we were using didn't get it. He was still taking the same old pictures from fifteen years ago. It wasn't working anymore, you know?

38

Me:	You said that you guys are very proactive. How can actors be more proactive in their careers? Because often people say well, I've got an agent. I don't need to do anything now.
David:	No, you're right. They do say that. We have our actors get in workshops. We have them get in showcases. We have them constantly updating their resume. Taking their pictures, going around to the casting facilities and dropping their headshots off. That stuff— some people like it and some don't. Some casting directors don't mind it at all.

It's very important these days to be putting videos and little sketches or skits, or whatever you want to call them, online. And that's being proactive. We love when people do that because we use those things. Half the time the casting directors don't have a lot of time to look at a five minute sketch, but you know what? Sometimes they do and we've gotten people auditions and even book stuff because they have things on LA Casting and Casting Frontier that are sketches, or even stand-up routines. That's being proactive.

It's very easy to sit around and blame your agent once you get one. "Heh! My agent's not doing this, my agent's not doing that." You know what? You've got stuff to do, too! Say we have a client who is one of our steady bookers and hasn't booked in two years. We tell them, "You know what? Get in a workshop. Maybe you're pushing too much." It happens all the time, and they'll go to a workshop and they'll see themselves and go, "You know what? I was pushing too much!" Or they see themselves and they'll say, "Oh my God I didn't know I did that," and, "That's new, I never did that before! Maybe that's the reason I'm not booking!"

Keep busy. Stay in workshops, stay in the classes,

send the postcards out, tell them when you booked a guest star on something... you booked a guest-star on CSI? Send a postcard out. They don't go unnoticed. They might not stick it up on their bulletin board but it gets to their desk. That I promise.

Me: Do you think that it's easier now because the advances of social media that actors—

David: Yes, yes, we signed a couple of people from their work on YouTube!

Me: What is your biggest challenge in what you do?

David: Wow, that's a tough one... it's not a challenge to book people. I guess the biggest challenge would be getting the casting director to see someone they don't want to see. That's a challenge. That's probably the thing I deal with most of the day-to-day— not every day, but once or a couple times a week— and it's great when that person turns around and becomes one of their favorites. It's happened many times. Casting directors— you need their trust. That's a challenge sometimes. You need the casting director's trust. I've been working with some [casting directors] for fifteen years so they trust me, but others are new. They creep up all the time. They're spin-offs, if you will, of all the older casting directors. The assistants and the associates are now casting directors and if I don't know them... Almost all the casting directors we work with were assistants at one point.

                [Some can be] tough but [some] will call me and say, "Listen, get me your best three comedians for this," and they'll give me three slots and trust me to fill them in, won't question me. They'll say, "OK great." I've earned that with some casting directors.

Me: What do you love about your job?

David: I love when actors work. Hopefully we at the agency
          can change the financial situation for an actor if he
          books a great gig or if she books a great gig. I love the
          interaction with the clients every day. I love talking
          to the casting directors. I love meeting new potential
          clients. I love looking at pictures. I mean literally—
          almost everything I do— I really enjoy. It's not a job
          where I wake up and go, "Man, I got to go to work
          today." You know? It's like, "Yay, I'm going to work!
          It's going to be a fun day." Otherwise I wouldn't
          have been doing this for fifteen years. I would have
          certainly moved on by now.

Me: What is your biggest pet peeve?

David: Laziness! No question about it. The worst! Very
          simple things like your resumé. Keep your resumé
          updated. That's a pet peeve when actors don't do it.

          And excuses! Why they can't make auditions— pet
          peeve. But the biggest one is laziness. People don't
          want to go and audition in Santa Monica because it's
          during rush hour and they don't want to get stuck in
          traffic? I hate that! I've heard that so many times…
          That's a really bad reason. I get on the phone when
          I hear something like that and say, "Really? There's
          500,000 other people who would be happy to get in
          their car to go to this audition." There're so many
          actors here. Someone could take their place. Easily.

Me: What can actors do to stand out, be more unique
          so they can get more auditions? Maybe even more
          bookings?

David: Listen, it all depends… we just told someone today, it's
          not going to be about your acting. You're a good actor.
          You're doing a really good job with it. We met two
          people today and they were both great. This is clearly
          a question of where they're going to fit in on our client
          list. They were both twenty-five to thirty. They were

41

both in the heaviest portion of our list. We have the most people between twenty-five and thirty-five, but at the same time I love new faces, you know? So what can they do to stand out is be on their game. Be as good as you can be as an actor and have a wonderful personality.

We've gone in that room and there's people that we're doing a favor for— a manager or something, or a casting director— and we all go in kind of dragging our heads and just not into it. So we'll make it real fast, make a real fast interview. And then we end up being in there for half an hour because the person was so much fun and entertaining! We end up signing them. And on the flip side, we're excited to meet someone that's with another agency— they've got five national network commercials on the air— and they're a drip. They come so highly recommended and they're horrible! It's like getting blood from a stone to get them to answer questions. So we passed.

Me: What is one piece of advice you can give to an actor just starting out?

David: Let's see actors starting out... for commercials... actors starting out should take workshops. They should take acting classes. They should get themselves in a showcase of some sort. They should get great headshots. That's one of the most important things. Their headshots have to really stand out. I'll tell you what... we met a girl today whose headshot wasn't great. As a matter of fact, I told her when I looked at her headshot, I went, "Hmm." That was my reaction. Then when I met her I said, "You need new pictures. You need new pictures because if you just sent this in to me in the mail and I opened it up, I would put it in a pile of people I don't need to see." Truthfully it just wasn't good, so headshots are the most important thing... get them.

It doesn't mean you have to spend a thousand dollars. There are great headshot photographers out there that will charge $350 to $400. You also don't want look great for commercials in every picture. You don't want them to look touched up and perfect. How many commercials do you see character people who haven't shaved in six days and, you know, look kind of scruffy and stuff like that, you know? Even for the women playing a character part... you don't want to look great and people think they have to look great in all the pictures. It works against them.

And hustle... really hustle. Don't just sit back and expect the phone to ring because I promise you it will not. I was an actor years ago and I was spoiled because I was getting all these roles in college and even some of the professors were asking me to be in their plays they were directing. I rarely had to audition for anything my senior year. I'm not sure I auditioned for anything. I wasn't an idiot and I knew it would be a little difficult, the difference anyway, when I moved to New York. But I was complacent. I was just lazy. It's just nothing happened for me. And you can't be lazy. That's one thing I stress! You cannot be lazy! And there's a lot of luck involved too.

Actors go out on hundreds of auditions before they book a job. They might book a job that is a great spot, that's with a celebrity, and it never runs. They make no money. It's a real crapshoot. It's a numbers game and I'm sure you've heard it a million times.

Me: Any advice for a seasoned actor?

David: You know, if you feel like you're in a slump then get yourself into a workshop and make sure your headshots are updated, make sure your resumé's updated... And continue practicing. Listen, it's not brain surgery, let's face it. Half the commercials don't have dialogue... it's a look.

Keep reinventing yourself. We had a kid today that came in. He had a bad haircut for a long time. He came in today, and I swear to God, an hour ago, and showed me his new haircut. I said this is going to help. Let's get new pictures. Let's start rocking and rolling here. He had a dated look from, like, the seventies like Kenny Loggins. He was too old, it wasn't working anymore, and he cut his hair to a modern 2013 hairstyle, and we're going to take new pictures. He reinvented himself.

Bob McGowan,
Talent Manager, McGowan Management

Bob McGowan has been a personal manager for over 25 years, among his first clients were Kim Delany and *Sopranos* star, Tony Sirico, whom he still represents. Bob has built the careers of many of today's stars, including Julia Roberts, whom he discovered (but no longer manages), Maria Bello, Dylan Walsh, Teri Polo, and Jesse L. Martin.

Bob has also been a personal friend of mine for over a decade, and is one of the most down-to-earth, approachable, and iconic guys in the industry. He offers an insight to the industry that would make for a great novel. Although his perspective may be different from others, you'll see that there are a lot of similarities in some of his answers to some of the other interviews. In fact, you'll see that throughout this book.

Me:	How often do you take clients on with little or no credits?
Bob:	If they're young, I'm willing to take a chance on them with no credits. Young meaning seventeen, eighteen.
Me:	Is that because you think that it's easier for people with no credits to break in when they're younger rather than when they're older?
Bob:	Absolutely. If they're older it's almost impossible. I'll give you an example. We met a girl, not too long ago. She was thirteen. She came walking in here with her mother and her lawyer. She only had a couple of credits. We sent her on an audition— the show called *Big Love*— and she got it. There's stories like that, but for every story like that, there's a thousand stories not like that.
	People just start so young now. What I tell people, when parents call me about their kids— they're about to go to college and they want to get involved in

acting— I tell them if they want to pursue an acting career, go to a college or university either in New York or LA so they can pursue the acting thing while they're going to college. The acting thing meaning they can pursue an agent and audition. The mistake people make is they wait 'til they are twenty-two to start. That's tough because the competition is fierce.

Me: While in college or while pursuing their acting career when they're younger, or even at any age, how important is training? What kind of training do you look for if they have no credits?

Bob: Well, you're talking to somebody, to a manager who was never an actor, and my perspective is a lot different than other people. I was never on the creative end. When I started, I just threw people out there, but I've had a number of people who were actually high school dropouts and just about graduated high school that made it big. Julia Roberts is a perfect example. I met her when she was just out of high school. She never took an acting class in her life.

Then I had Teri Polo who was sixteen, who got a soap opera real quick, *Loving*, while she was studying at the William Esper Studio in New York. After a few months, she quit because she got a job on a soap, and then she's never stopped working. She's the girl in *Meet the Parents, Meet the Fockers*. She never studied.

On the other hand, Jesse Martin, who's won a number of awards, who was on *Law and Order* for years, he did study, but he didn't study acting. He went to NYU for management, or whatever financial career, and he ended up being an actor because he was auditioning while he was going to college.

I'm a believer of either you have it or you don't.

Me: What holds actors back from getting work in this

industry? Training or credits, or without training or credits? Because some people, even if they have credits, seem to struggle more than others that may not.

Bob: I think there's a lot of luck involved in it. What I tell clients of mine, I want them to work as hard as I do. There's a lot of things that they can do to help their own career. For example, there's a lot of good actors that are lousy auditioners, so they should go to audition classes.

A lot of them don't. There's actors that are still trying to get started that have never gone to an audition class. There's actors that studied for years that didn't take audition classes. It's a whole different thing.

Me: In what ways can actors be more proactive about their own careers? We've talked about them taking an audition class or classes where they're lacking certain skills. What other types of things can they do?

Bob: They can be more proactive by having an up-to-date headshot. What's happening now, only in recent years, is when you submit… everything's electronic. You submit a headshot electronically. You have a little reel to go with it and that reel has to be constantly up-to-date. There's got to be something funny on it, something dramatic. Actors have to really try to get that. If they don't have real work, they've got to go out and do a scene and put it on the reel. That's one thing they can do.

Me: How different is the business now as compared to when you started 28 years ago? How have you seen it develop over this last couple of decades?

Bob: There's a lot more managers now, that's for sure. It's different in a way. There are a lot more opportunities though, too. Years ago, there was never Showtime, The CW, HBO, and all that, so they create more jobs.

The downside is there's tons of reality shows now, which I'm not crazy about. They're the major changes in the business.

The basic rules are still the same. Actors have to go audition, they've got to get the casting directors and if casting directors like them, they call them back. The basics are still the same, but the changes— I mean there's less movies now, but there's a lot more TV.

Me: How about the online presence? Do you think that is a good opportunity for actors?

Bob: Yes, absolutely!

Me: What is your biggest challenge in what you do?

Bob: I'm at a point now where I have established clients, and I have a lot of people on shows. I just basically do the same ... when you say it's a challenge ... I look forward to coming to work every day. If I ever had to go get a real job, I wouldn't know what to do. So I don't really see it as a challenge. I love calling a client up and telling them on the phone that they got a job. That's a great thrill for me whether it's big or little.

Me: What do you love about actors?

Bob: I admire the fact that they can take all the rejection they take, because 98% of this business is rejection. And if you can't take rejection you shouldn't be in this business. I admire that about them.

Me: I know you've had some pretty amazing stories...

Bob: Actually, here's a story from not too long ago. Across from my office there's a little restaurant. I'm sitting in there one day by myself in the back reading a script, and I get a call from a casting director, Judy Wilson, from *All my Children*. She calls me up on my cell phone, and she said, "Bob, do you have any Kim

48

Basinger types?" She said, "I know your clients don't do soap operas but you might have somebody new that's interested". I said, "Wait a minute. My clients do soap operas," so I said, "What are you looking for?" She described it to me, and as I'm talking to her, I'm looking at this girl who's the hostess who I don't know. I said to Judy the casting director, "Let me call you back." I walked up to [the hostess], and she has seen me come in there over the last few months, but I'd never talked to her. I walked up to her and I said, "Excuse me," I said, "you know, I'm married, I'm not trying to hit on you. Are you an actress?" Well she looked like Kim Basinger. She said, "Yeah but I'm brand new." I said, "Do you have an agent?" She said, "No." I said, "Well wait five minutes." I went back, I called up Judy the casting director, and I told her, "There's this girl looks just like Kim Basinger. I don't know if she can act, but she's an aspiring actress." She said, "Well lets set her up." So, they saw her, they put her on tape, they sent the tape to New York.

To make a long story short, she got a three-year contract, making like four or five hundred thousand a year, and was nominated for a number of Emmys over a few years, and right now as of today, she just started on the *Young and the Restless*, because *All My Children* was canceled. She's a big soap star now. Her name's Melissa Clair Egan. She played Annie on *All my Children*. I think that's a great story. It's another example of so much luck involved, and being in the right place at the right time.

When I got Julia Roberts here, she was eighteen, and the reason I got her was, there was an agent in New York, medium-sized agency, and they were trying to help me. I was a relatively new manager, and she said, "Bobby we have this girl, her name's Julie,"— not even Julia— "her name's Julie Roberts and she's Eric Roberts' younger sister. She's too green for us but we know you're looking for new young clients. Would you be interested in meeting her?" And I did. My thing back then was if somebody was that young and gorgeous and wanted to be with me, great. I had her for a number of years. I had her up until Pretty Woman, and she was great.

Me: So, you're saying there is a lot of luck involved, and basically, in order to get lucky, people need to hang out where you are?

Bob: (Laughing)

Me: What's the best advice you can give to actors just starting out?

Bob: The best advice is just be dedicated.

Me: What's the best advice you can give to actors just starting out who are older?

Bob: Well, it's going to depend on their look, whether they're a lady, men, or character... but be the best. Do as much as you can for yourself, like submit yourself to things to help you get an agent, because a good agent or a good manager as a rule, is not going to take you if you're older and just starting out. It's just a lot of work. And I would just try to get to know as many people as you can. There's a new thing going on in the last four or five years, which is good for *anybody* starting out to do. These casting directors have these workshops— this is all new, new to me anyway— and they're all doing it! I would take these workshops to get to know the casting directors and the assistant casting directors. They do bring you in on things after you take their workshop, because they know you.

Jerry Silverhardt,
Talent Manager

Jerry began his career in the entertainment industry because of his mother, who owned a nightclub. When he was still a kid, he had come home from school one day and his mother told him he had to start "booking the room." He didn't know what that meant at the time, but he figured it out pretty quickly. He had booked acts like The Drifters and The Shirells.

While working for Bantam Books in the late '70s, Jerry was at a convention where he met the legendary Melba Moore, who had no manager at the time. He was a huge fan, and he got to know her very well over time, and booked her on a few symphony gigs.

One evening, at a dinner with Ms. Moore and her office manager, the 24 year old Jerry Silverhardt officially became Melba's manager, getting her back on Broadway.

Jerry has since discovered and managed Tom Cruise, Dylan McDermott, and Richard Greico, among many other notable actors.

Me: How did you come to rep Tom Cruise?

Jerry: Sweetest kid in the world, lived in New Jersey, graduated high school in New Jersey but came from Louisville, Kentucky. He had a smile— still does— that would light up an entire theatre. I don't remember the timeline, I don't know if he had done his first or second movie. He did a movie called *Taps*.

Me: That was with Timothy Hutton.

Jerry: And Sean Penn.

I'm going to tell you the great story about that movie that probably no one knows. He got cast in a different role. The role you know is not the one he had. He had a smaller role. We were in Valley Forge, Pennsylvania. The director was Harold Becker, young in the field. The producers were Stanley Jaffe, who at one point,

51

ran Columbia Pictures, Sherry Lansing before she was the president of Paramount.

It was in Valley Forge, they're rehearsing and I get a call from Stanley Jaffe. I'm thinking he's getting fired, right? Why else would he call? "Hi, this is Stanley Jaffe." "Hi, Mr. Jaffe." "You can call me Stanley." I couldn't. He came from a very famous family. I'm ready to think of the worst, so I'm ready to make excuses. I almost started to say, "He's a good kid, he's brand new." I said, " How can I help you?"

Stanley said, "Well, there's a little problem with Tommy." I'm like, uh-oh, here it comes. I say, "What's the problem?" He said, "Well, during rehearsals we've seen Tommy and he's really good, he's got it. There's a boy in the movie who has the role of Dave and he can't cut it."

I said, "So what's the problem with Tommy?" He says, "We want to flip-flop the roles. We want Tommy to take over the role of Dave and the kid that's playing Dave take the role of Tommy." I say, "What's the problem?" He says, "Tommy won't do it because he doesn't want to hurt his friend."

I said, "Oh, wow. I can talk to Tommy." He says, "This is what you need to tell him. If he doesn't take the role of Dave, he stays in his role and the boy playing Dave we're going to replace. He'll be out of the movie entirely. If he does allow us to flip flop the roles, at least his friend will still work on the entire movie. He'll be in the movie and he'll still get paid."

I call Tommy. After the talk he decided— because when I said to him, "Tommy, you know that guy… if you don't do it, you'll stay in your role and your friend will not be in the movie. He will not be making that paycheck." He didn't want to see his friend get fired.

Me: How long did you represent him?

52

Jerry:	I had him all the way until after *Risky Business*.
Me:	That's the one that made him a star.
Jerry:	I also got him in *The Outsiders*.

When they were casting *Risky Business* the casting director wasn't initially going to bring him in because he didn't believe that anyone would believe a good-looking boy like a Tom Cruise as a virgin. I was tenacious and got him the movie, and that was his defining role.

And then Dylan McDermott I found at The Neighborhood Playhouse. I was friends with his aunt or aunt-in-law. It was one of those— "My nephew is an actor." Then she said to me he's in a scene at the neighborhood class. I'd love for you to come.

He then got to be the first replacement in Neil Simon's *Biloxi Blues*. Then he did his first movie, *Hamburger Hill*.

Me:	Wow! When you're looking for talent now, what is it that you're looking for? Are you looking for credits, are you looking for people who are younger? What specifically draws you to a client, especially one that might be unknown?
Jerry:	Well now I'm not as keen into getting unknowns anymore. Not just unknowns, I mean somebody without a credit. Because it's getting harder and harder to get someone in the room.

I look for spark, sparkle, personality, someone who looks smart. I mean every now and then if I attend a workshop and I get to do a Q&A, I always talk about how important it is for an actor to be well-read, because you can't imagine how many actors and actresses I've met who don't read.

No clue since they got out of school, not only just read books… how about the papers, how about a magazine? I try to tell them that when you go into a room you might have that one person that's going to ask that question that you're not going to answer because why? You're not well read.

Me: Has that happened before?

Jerry: Yeah. I was at a workshop in and I signed this guy that I'm really excited about. He met these agents the other day who I love, who was blown away because the conversation got into the place that I always talk about. First it was a little about politics, and then they said you know, "Do you have a favorite author, anything you're currently reading?"

            It doesn't always happen, but every now and then it does come up. I believe that's going to help you be a better actor, because you're dealing with what's going on. You know what's going on in the world, so you have something to draw from.

Me: In looking for people who are well read or at least have a pulse on what's going on in the world, how important is training if they don't have credits?

Jerry: Very important. It's funny you said that. Not too long ago I had a client who had got back to me that he was no longer in a class. I said to him, "How come you're not? First of all you didn't tell me— not good; second of all why would you stop going to class?" He's saying to me it's financially whatever, and that usually is keynote to being an excuse, unfortunately.

            "Well I don't need it right now."

            You don't need it right now? Why? You're in demand when? I believe an actor should always be in a class. I don't believe an actor should never *not* be in a class.

When I had Dylan as a client he did *Golden Boy* at the Williamstown Theater Festival and the director was Joanne Woodward. Everybody was at that opening! Tom Dean Green, Paul Newman, Amy Irving, Spielberg.

The reason I bring it up… they did these Sunday cabaret things or homages. They did an homage to The Neighborhood Playhouse. They filmed it for PBS, by the way, and it was incredible because the stage was filled with everybody that had at some point been in The Neighborhood Playhouse.

We're talking about Comden and Green, who were big Broadway show writers, we're talking about Sidney Kingsley who wrote the *Dead End Kids*. We're talking about Ruth Nelson, not that she was ever a star but worked a lot on Broadway, did a few movies. On Broadway she was the original Mona June in *Golden Boy*. She was the original female lead. Cut to few years later she does the movie *Awakenings* playing De Niro's mother.

Me: Wow.

Jerry: Joanne, Paul Newman, Kate Burton, Shelly Winters were on stage in this. Everybody. Ellen Burstyn. It was amazing, and they all said the same thing: they still go to class! Ellen Burstyn and Shelly Winters were talking about how they, once a month or whatever, go to the Actor's Studio, they check in and they're working on a scene. They put up a scene!

This is why I say this! Even just recently I said it in the workshop I was at. I said, "Ellen Burstyn has won an Oscar, a Tony and I think an Emmy. I said, "If she can still work on a scene, then who are you?" That's my total belief. I don't ever want to hear someone telling me, "I'm not in class, I need a break." Unless you're working on a movie or you're in a series every week, then I get it.

Me:	What in your opinion holds actors back from getting work in this industry?
Jerry:	Sometimes the bull they bring in the room with them.
Me:	Like what?
Jerry:	Problems from "the outside world." Funny, this workshop I did Sunday there were two wonderful casting directors I love. They brought this up, right? "You've got to understand when you walk in the room," this one casting lady said, "I know what's going on. Your job is whatever it is that you have got going on, you have to leave it outside the door." She said, "Not outside the door of the casting room but before you walk into the reception area— shake it out."
	I said to a client if that means bringing your little iPod and listening to something nice and looking at your material, then that's something you need to do. You need to take yourself out of that outside world and put yourself into this. That's a big problem with actors and that keeps actors from working.
	The other thing is ego. And another thing is not wanting to work.
Me:	What do you mean not wanting to work?
Jerry:	They don't want to work on their craft.
	I was on the phone with a casting director and she was saying that how many times actors come in and they're not totally prepared, or she hears them gossiping in the waiting room instead of [focusing on the audition]. It doesn't mean you have to work on the material in the waiting room, but you should be just tuning in to what you need to be doing.
	My other client who's done a lot of TV, she was on the

Star Trek series with Patrick Stewart. She's English. Her name is Marina Sirtis. She was also in the movie *Crash*— she went in for a movie for Marvel Films. They do the read and then Marina said, "Do you want to see me do it in another way?"

"No, you so nailed it." She was working on the material.

I think too many actors get in their own way.

Me: How different is the business now?

Jerry: There were not a million casting directors. I think a lot of casting directors in the old days had a great foundation. Coming out of theatre schools, really watching movies, coming out of a really good casting office, the old school.

Way back then I'd go to Warner Brothers, I'd go to Marty James at Universal and I walk in with, like, a portfolio of clients and, "Okay, we'll put them on tape in New York." That's how you did it. There was nothing like [online submission], and it was more that you were in touch.

I get why they do online, but it's sad because it's so impersonal. I get that they say there are a thousand managers and agents and they can't talk to everybody, but it's impersonal. Well how do you build a relationship?

Me: Do you find that it's harder?

Jerry: It is hard. I have to keep relying on my relationships that I've had over time.

Me: Because everything has become more impersonal with the online stuff, do you think that because it's so much easier to submit online that there are just more actors being submitted for every role now?

Jerry:	One casting director once said to me, "You don't understand, Jerry. I click on this role in the breakdown and there's like eight, nine hundred actors." I said to him, "Do you look at all of the submissions?" He goes, "No, I can't." That's scary.
Me:	How, then, would someone like you get an actor in for a meeting?
Jerry:	I have relationships with casting directors. Even the ones that say absolutely no phone calls, if I know them well enough... and the assistant says to me, "You know on the breakdown it says no phone calls..." I know they're not talking about me. I have relationships with a lot of the network casting people, and that helps.
Me:	So you call in and you pitch your clients?
Jerry:	Oh yeah, but I pick my battles.
Me:	Do you find that the clients you pitch, do they tend to get called back more or booked more?
Jerry:	Yeah.
Me:	What strategies do you try to practice when representing a new comer or someone with very little credits or have you in the past since you're not doing it so much now?
Jerry:	If they don't have a lot of credits I tend to really submit them more on co-stars. For me, that gets their foot in the door, they have a better shot at it, they have a better shot at getting the appointment and then if they book the job, they're learning and they get a credit and you can get some footage. That's usually what I do. Every now and then, if I think they're so right on for a guest star role— but if it's too "top tier," that's not going to happen because I know the casting director won't bring in someone that basically doesn't

have credits because they're going to think that they're too green, and you have never worked in front of a camera.

It's just like when they're casting a half hour, there's multi-camera, which is in front of the audience. Then there's single film, and a lot of actors don't know how to work multi-camera. There are certain casting directors that won't bring you in if you haven't done multi-camera. That means you have to know how to work that camera, who's on and who's not and who to play to and who not to play to. That's hard.

Half hour is now coming back right now because of *Modern Family* and because *The New Girl*. There's more opportunities that can happen but they'll do more half hours this season and pilots. I'm sure of it.

Me: Can you describe your role in working with agents, and how you work together?

Jerry: When my clients are with an agent we're there for the same purpose, we're working for the same good, as good as it could be. I will always say to an agent if I have a new relationship with them, maybe the client has been with the agent before me that I'm only here to augment everything. We could both submit ... "I don't care who gets the appointment as long as you get my client in the door."

I say, "Listen, if you're having a hard time let me know because I have a relationship with that casting director, so we'll double team." That is usually very good. Or maybe I can call the network. I won't do it on guest roles, of course. Or maybe I can call the head of casting at the studio. I try to do a group effort at times, unfortunately that doesn't always work.

We have small lists so I try to concentrate on the big picture, the entire picture from photos... kind of like mentoring them. I mean I come from the old school, I'm a *personal* manager.

If I'm working with an agent that kind of has my sensibility it makes it easier

Me: What's your biggest challenge in what you do as a personal manager?

Jerry: My business is very good in beating you up… Not losing a client. Small agencies and managers that are not at the big companies, we all are at the mercy of a bigger agency or a bigger management company. I had a client that I had basically discovered— he had no credit but I'm passionate about who I represent. He got a small role in a movie, then he got role in another movie, then the movie got to Sundance and he started getting heat. From that he got something else, and then he got a pilot with Rob Morrow, a half hour.

I got him a good agency and then they said he was getting an offer for a pilot. I got him up for a really good movie— a studio movie with a major director and a major star— and it was a nice supporting role. Here's the kick. They called the agent with two separate projects and the agent says— when he we knew he was getting the pilot— [the agent] just randomly says to the producer on the movie [the actor] can't do both. Without even trying to work [the schedule] out! Well, I understand part of it was because the pilot is shot here and the movie was shooting in New York but he didn't make an attempt.

Only by the grace of God I called the movie to see what was going on, because I kept hearing he was getting the offer. They said, "Well you know, Jerry, I think it's going south." I said, "Why is it going south?"

"Well, the agent said…" I go, "What did the agent say?"

"Well he just said your client is not going to be available," and all that, but no one talked to each other. What I did was, I got the line producer of the movie on the phone with the production manager of the pilot and they were able to make it work!

Of course at that time the kid goes, "You're amazing." He got both jobs. Movie comes out, the pilot doesn't get picked up, then he does something else and does something else... Then he got a big studio movie. Not a starring role, but he got an important movie, an important director...

He goes off and does the movie, comes back, he gets the movie of the week, a name kid is in it, the named kid's manager is on the set. At that time I was not at a company, I was working on my own out of my house and this actor is, like, "I'm so afraid I'm not going to work again," and he fires me to go to a bigger company because it's all glamorous.

I've always worked. I'm like, "I don't know, man, while you were with me you almost went job to job to job and you just finished this big movie."

Fires me. I'm devastated.

He goes to the big company... he sat for almost a year. He did one guest role and he did a little movie, and the little movie happened to be my friend producing it. That's kind of how he got it. He was up for the movie with Bill Macy and they were on the fence, and my friend called me up and said, "Do you want me to put him in the movie [or not]?"

I would never do that. I said, "Honestly, I think he'd be brilliant in that role," and he gets the movie. He comes crawling back to me, I take him back.

He's with me for a couple of years, he gets a series, we go to New York for the upfronts, we come home, he starts the series. It's well off and running. We're getting ready for a Christmas break, he really wants to work on his hiatus to do a movie or something. I go to the coffee shop, and I'm sitting all day long reading scripts, my eyes are burning, but that's what you do.

We stack up for the first year and it was one or two weeks later we're at the People's Choice Awards, and the network sends us in a limo, everything is fine, goes back onto the show, hiatus is done, calls me on the phone a week later to fire me— not in person— and said to me, "You know I don't like doing this, I love you like a brother." I said, "And you're firing me? Because of what?"

"Well you know, I want to make sure I have a movie on my hiatus and there's another big company and they promised me."

I'm like, "Really?" Anyway, the end of the story is he didn't get a movie, the movie didn't get produced like he wanted, he did the series for six years. He never had a job on any hiatus for six years.

Why do you think? He didn't lose his talent. [It's because] there's no one passionate behind him. No one worked with him like I worked with him, because they had 50 other clients on their list and that's the way it is.

That's always the fear: I'm going to pop another kid, he's going to take off and we get screwed. It happens all the time. It's kind of the beast of the.

Me: What should actors never do out there?

Jerry: Dress like bums. I just think at a certain point for an actor that appearance is important even when they're not working. I don't mean they have to wear suits or anything, but I get tired of seeing them dressed like schlubs. That's just me. I'm from the old world. I think the other thing... it's funny, again, because I am from the old world. When I go to premieres and parties with clients, if there's going to be a picture taken, I take the glass away because I also see you being a role model and I think it's just not okay. Call me old fashioned. That's why I like when I'm watching a talk show— I love watching people like Clooney and Matt Damon and Ben Affleck, because when they come on the show they look like movie stars! Versus someone that's coming on with ripped jeans.

I just think it's just not good. I think out there they should be more respectful, I think they shouldn't be getting high. They should be aware that people are watching them all the time. Even when you're not a star somebody is always going to remember you.

Me: What's your biggest pet peeve then?

Jerry: Please call or email me after a meeting or audition so I know how it went. Don't tell me three days later. More importantly, because if they feel it didn't go well and I know then, then maybe I can adjust it, maybe I can get you back in the room. If you're going to call me three or four days later there's nothing I can do anymore.

My thing that I always tell clients is, "When you go in that room, those two or three minutes, that's your time in there." You do the meeting, the casting director might say, "Oh good," and you say to him, "Do you think I can do it another way or do you mind if I run it up one more time?" I say that gives you the chance to do it again. They're not going to always say yes, but if one out of six says yes, you're ahead of the game. Instead of saying to me, "I could have done it this other way, I should have, could have, would have..." I don't want to hear it. Make that moment in that room work for you.

I always say to them be respectful to [the casting director] no matter if they're paying attention or not—because that does happen sometimes.

Me: How long do you stick with an actor who may not be pulling his or her weight?

Jerry: I don't have a time limit. It just depends. I just say to them, "Maybe you need to change it up, maybe you need to be in another class," which I think is important. Those are the things I do. I'm there to help them. I don't kick somebody if they're down, but if I see a constant pattern then I start rethinking the situation. If I'm giving them the advice how to maybe make it better and they're not paying attention, then we have a talk and maybe I'll have to let them go.

Hey, you either want it or you don't.

You're not calling me, you're not staying in touch with me and then the next thing I hear from someone you get another tattoo? You got to ask me first you got run it by me. You're going to get piercings up and down your ear and just think it's okay? It's not okay. Then if that happens then I let them go.

It's funny… I was with a bunch of managers the other day we were saying no one wants to let anybody go anymore. Every now and then you hear about a story where someone says I got this client for four years, hardly worked but I worked my ass off, I dropped him and what do you think happened? They get the lead in a series.

Me: How many clients do you have on your roster now?

Jerry: I have two screenwriters, so including my two writers I have 12 clients.

Me: Ten actors, two writers?

Jerry:	Yeah.
Me:	What's the best advice you can give an actor just starting out?
Jerry:	Study, study, study, get into class, get into class, get into class.
Me:	How about a nice piece of advice for a seasoned actor?
Jerry:	Stay in class, stay in class, stay in class. You're always learning. The other thing is, when I go, "What's your favorite show," [and they say,] "Well I don't really watch TV..."

And you're an actor? How can you not watch TV, how can you not go to the movies? That's another pet peeve of mine. I'm always saying, "If this is what you want, you got to immerse yourself into it."

I'm not saying you have to watch every show every week [but] watch every show at least twice so you know what's out there, so if you get an audition you know what you're doing.

Do your homework, watch one episode of either the producer or the show you're going in on so you know what the tone is and you know what to expect. You're ahead of the game when you do your homework. When a client says, "Well I didn't get to watch it last night," go on Hulu! You're going to always find it, so watch it. That's my other piece of advice.

Me:	Any last words of inspiration for people who are starting out?
Jerry:	Embrace your craft and embrace yourself and you can do well. That's the other thing I think a lot of actors have a problem with. Know who you are, look in the mirror, see who you are. Maybe you're not the leading man, you're not the ingénue, but embrace who you

are and make that work for you, instead of if you're definitely not the leading man and you're calling up your agent and your manager going, "How come I'm not going in on the Ryan Gosling roles or the Ryan Reynolds?" Well, let me see... You're pudgy, you're not the leading man. However, you could have a career like Ned Beatty, you could have a career like Charles Durning.

Know who you are and embrace who you are, and that helps an actor have a career.

TJ Stein,
Talent Manager, Stein Entertainment

As a contrast to Bob and Jerry, who operate as independents, I briefly interviewed TJ Stein, owner of Stein Entertainment, a mid-size, but highly respected and influential management company. TJ has been known as the top kids manager in town, and he handles adults as well.

Me: How important is training, and what kind of training do you look for?

TJ: We like clients who have television credits, since it tells us the actor has been on a set. However, we are open to actors that might not have a credit but we see potential, talent and marketability. Training is essential. We read resumés from the bottom up, looking at their training. The type of training we look for are recognizable University Programs, Coaches that have been recognized in LA and NY are important. We like to see they have a variety of classes. On-Camera, Improv and Audition Technique are all important.

Me: What holds actors back from getting work?

TJ: Many actors seem to think they should be starring in a feature film and doing pilots within a few weeks of landing in LA. There is a reality to the fact that you have to make relationships and that takes time. There can be some situations where someone gets a Cinderella start, but that doesn't make for a career. Careers happen over time. Work takes work. I find many actors walk into our offices and tell us they have gotten themselves most of their work by themselves, that's an actor's job. Managers need something to manage. If you bring to the table something exciting, then we can use that to promote and pitch. This means, doing workshops, plays and marketing yourself. The more you do for yourself, the more your representation can do for you.

Me: In what way can actors and parents of child actors be more productive?

TJ: Communication, workshops, classes. Reading! Read plays, including the classics. I also love books like "Acting Is Everything" from Judy Kerr and Scott Sedita's great book on comedy, "The Eight Characters of Comedy."

Me: How different is the business now as compared to two, three, five years ago?

TJ: There's more work, there's more platforms, there's more opportunity. There's also more competition because of the Internet. We can find talent from small towns and have access to their auditions with the use of Internet which is very helpful.

Me: What's one of the biggest misconceptions actors and parents have about the business?

TJ: They will get rich quick! It's a long process and careers are like marathons, they are not a quick sprint!

Me: What does your typical day look like?

TJ: Busy! We are always busy in our offices. We have office meetings to discuss our goals and we work as a team in our office. All the clients are given our attention, we don't have one manager responsible for only some of the clients, we represent all the clients together. It allows us more creativity and support. We have meetings with clients, discuss career goals and meet new talent. We spend a lot of time reading scripts, pitching actors and discussing projects that we feel are right for the clients.

Me: What's you biggest challenge in what you do?

TJ: Actors need to trust their reps. It's hard when you have a client who doesn't understand we want everyone to have opportunity. We work for everyone equally. It's about trusting us— not challenging your representation. Ask what you can do to help as an actor and don't have unrealistic goals.

Me: What should actors and parents never do out there?

TJ: When you go to auditions, don't go to socialize, it's a job interview. Treat it as a professional experience.

Me: What's your biggest pet peeve?

TJ: Don't show up unprepared for a meeting, especially with our company. If you are coming into the office, dress appropriately. Look good and be professional. When an actor walks into our office and asks us questions that clearly show they have done no research— that they don't know anything about our company, or if we're Managers or Agents— that is always disappointing. Actors that don't prepare. Actors who are late.

Me: What's the biggest piece of advice you can give to actors just starting out, maybe their parents?

TJ: Training and positive attitude. If this were easy, everyone would do it because it's fun when you get to work. 90% of the actor's job is auditioning, be prepared. Take class, train!

Me: What's the best advice you can give the seasoned actor?

TJ: Get coached! Work your social media. Be professional on set!

Me: What's the biggest piece of advice for parents who want to get their kids into acting?

TJ: Don't be their Manager!

The Casting Directors

Mark Teschner,
Casting Director, General Hospital

A native New Yorker, Mark Teschner has been a casting director for over thirty years. He has been described by *Rolling Stone* magazine as "an actor's casting director," and *TV Guide* noted his "unparalleled track record for finding new talent." For the past twenty-four years, Teschner has been the casting director for ABC's *General Hospital*. For his work on the show he has received five Emmy Awards for Outstanding Achievement for a Casting Director for a Drama series, as well as an additional six nominations. Teschner is also a six-time recipient of the Artios Award for Outstanding Achievement in Daytime Drama Casting, given by the Casting Society of America, and has received 16 additional nominations. In addition to his work on *General Hospital*, he casts feature films including *Elephant White*, starring Kevin Bacon, *And They're Off*, and *The Philly Kid*.

Teschner has served four terms on the board for the Academy of Television Arts & Sciences, and is former vice-president of the Casting Society of America. Mark also truly loves actors.

Me: You're one of those rare people who not only has such an amazing memory, but you really truly love actors.

Mark: I do. I was once an actor.

Me: I remember your headshot with the mustache.

Mark: That was a very big miscalculation. [Laughs]

Me: You've been a casting director for over thirty years. What made you decide to go into casting?

Mark: I started young. I heard about an opening for a casting position, and I just literally knew on a gut level in that moment. I just knew that I felt like I had hit on something that gave me creative input at an early stage of a project. For the first two years, I literally starved and it didn't matter. I loved it. I would work

73

long hours for very little money and I didn't care. I knew that I had found what I loved doing.

When I started in casting, it was really a profession that, still, wasn't really in the lexicon of people what casting directors do. Now I noticed in my thirty years that there's become a total respect for it. We have three primetime Emmys in casting. We now have two daytime Emmys in casting. We're working on getting that academy award for casting, which has been a long time coming. Syracuse University just became an accredited program, hooked up with the CSA.

Now there are college students telling me they want to be a casting director. That's something that never existed. When I was in college it was a mystery. Now there's a profession. There's an awareness, so whenever I meet somebody that's interested in casting, I love to be helpful and guide them because it's a profession I want to encourage people follow. It's a difficult profession, but the rewards unbelievably satisfying.

Me: What's really amazing about having a career that spans thirty years, twenty-four on *General Hospital* plus all the spin-offs, you've gotten to see some of these actors grow up on the set and develop as human beings, and create this whole life for them. You've been the surrogate parent in a way. I'm sure that must be some kind of sense of joy and pride for you, as well just helping these people fulfill their dreams.

Mark: There definitely is a sense of pride in that. One of the really great things about *General Hospital* I love is I get to mix on the canvas because it's so broad— incredibly well known, seasoned, respected veteran actors, whether it be Billy D. Williams, Michael Lerner, Bruce Davis, and James Franco. Yet on that same canvas, there are actors where it's their first major job, and there's tremendous excitement in the discovery of a talent where there's a rawness and a potential there, and you see it come to fruition. I'll meet an actor and they'll be one of about three to five hundred that usually audition for a series regular role, and they'll get the role and it can be their first substantial job, or it can even be their *first* job.

Then I watch them grow from an artist finding their voice to growing in terms of both their craft and who they are as a human being. I do, on some level, feel like a surrogate parent as I watch these people grow up over four years or even longer if they stay. Then when they leave it's as if they're leaving the nest and it's exciting to see where they go from there. There is something about being a part of someone's destiny that is profound, and I don't take that responsibility lightly.

Me: When you are auditioning two to three to five hundred people for a role for a contract role, a series regular, what do you look for in a particular actor? Do they have to fit a right look? Is it more about the acting? Is it more about the training?

Mark: Every role has a unique challenge based on the specifications of that particular role. For me, the common denominator in every role is talent and complexity whether somebody is fifty, forty, or even fifteen. I'm looking for somebody where there's something going on on another level. Even the kids that we hire— the eleven and twelve year olds— have been very special. They've had something where there's really something going on. Amber Tamblyn was thirteen when she got this show, but she was thirteen going on thirty in terms of possessing this complexity in both her presence and work. We're looking for those kids.

There are a lot of good actors. That's not an issue but it's finding one that resonates on a different level, or that's going to take the role to another level. Is this going to be an actor that the audience is going to want to watch for years? That they're going to be invested in?

There are other elements that go into casting. The sex appeal, the charisma, the presence depending on the role. Those have to be factored in. I always tell people that have this naïve assumption that "the look is everything" that they're really mistaken. The halls of casting directors are littered with photos and resumes of beautiful men and women who are not substantial actors who never get beyond that first reading. A great look will get you in the door but it won't necessarily keep you in the room. I'm big on studying. Through the years, the idea of what is sexy and dynamic has changed.

I'm looking for that combination of presence, charisma, appeal. But talent is going to be the hook day in and day out.

Me: You've won so many Emmys and Artios awards...

Mark: The awards, I can't pretend that they're not nice to look at, but I don't try to win an award. It's nice to be acknowledged. For me, the ultimate is when I'm watching the show and I see a scene and there's something magnificent going on and it makes me feel like I did my job because those are the right people right there. Seeing the audience respond to them and seeing them bring these scenes to life, that's ultimately where the reward has to lie, separate from anything.

Me: Aside from the series regular roles and the contract roles, when you're calling in people for under-fives or day-players, can you talk about that? How does an actor prepare for a role like that, and what are you looking for in those types of roles?

Mark:	I think that for an under-five, you have to just have a point of view about what the scene is about and just bring the truth to the scene. I think part of that is you have to know who you are, not just as an actor, but as a person. When you walk into the room, there's a sense of your presence being felt, and then just play the truth of the scene. Sometimes that's a visceral thing. Where there are a lot of people who can play those roles, we're also, maybe, looking for a specific look for that particular role.

When you get into the day players and the recurring roles, they're really substantial parts. We don't think there's any part that doesn't have importance on the show, whether it's one line or multiple scenes. I'm looking for something interesting that serves the scene.

I want somebody that has a point of view, that's going to challenge the actors on the set, that is going to be a worthy tennis opponent in that scene. I hire some incredible actors to come in— even for a day or two or three— and I want them to really bring a scene to life. I want them to be interesting. I want them to be compelling. We've had a couple of instances where actors that I brought in for three or four days were so interesting and unique that the writers responded to them, and they stayed on the show for much longer.

I'll give specific examples. We had an actress, Andrea Bogart, who came in to play the role of Abby. It was a two-day part of a beautiful stripper who befriends a young man who's naïve and challenged romantically. It was a complex part, and the writers responded to her and she was on the show for over a year. She became the love interest to that actor.

Robert LaSardo is a well known character actor and we had a bad guy part coming up for four days, and he was going to be killed. I was a huge fan of

Nip/Tuck, and he was the villain on the whole first season. I had him come in for four days and after the first day, the writers called me and said we don't want to kill this guy. Would he stay around? He became our main villain for almost two years.

Not that it happens all the time, but it's really great when an actor is cast and there is something so unique and compelling that it captures the imagination of the writers and producers in a way that takes it in a direction that wasn't planned. That's when I really feel like I've struck gold with those parts.

Me: What are some of the factors that actors may or may not know about that either get them the job or does not get them the job? There's certain mystique about auditioning sometimes. You're saying you look for this quality that is special, but are there actual things in— not necessarily who they are— but in how they read? Because you're also known for working with actors to bring out the best in them.

Mark: Certain actors just have a presence, a charisma where they're just very compelling, and the moment they walk in the room, you're hoping they're going to be as good as you need them to be just by virtue of who they are before they even read. That's that indefinable thing. It's a very exciting feeling when somebody walks in the room and you really respond to them and they back it up with their work. It's a little disappointing when somebody walks in the room and there's something very interesting and dynamic in their presence, but their work is flat or one-note. I think the best advice I can give to an actor is don't come into a room and make it about your auditioning.

Come in as a confident human being— and I say confident, not cocky— and view this as your opportunity to play the role for three minutes. Just bring in the confidence of somebody that has a point of view about the material, has made choices, is confident in their work, and just do the work as if you're just doing the scene, as if you have the job, as opposed to coming in needing a job. When an actor comes in needing the job or making the work about trying to please me, they're giving up something of themselves and they lose a little bit of that element. Some actors have that innately, that confidence— when they walk in the room— about their work regardless of how old or how experienced they are.

There really is a marked different between somebody that brings that into the room and somebody that is trying to get a job. There are so many factors that go into the casting beyond just the work. You just might not be right for the role so you can't come in "to get the job." You can only come in the room to do good work.

Me: That's a great point that you bring up, that so many actors, when they don't get a callback or they don't get the job, they think they did a terrible audition. Sometimes, they can do a good job they're just not right for the role.

Mark: I've auditioned actors where the an actor who was right for the part, read for it and didn't get a callback. They weren't right for the role. There are elements that go into casting that have to do with look, presence, sensibility. If I'm looking for a rough, edgy, blue-collar guy, and somebody comes in and reads and that's not their vibe or sensibility, they're not going to get the role regardless of how wonderful they are. But they might get something down the road. They may resonate with me for other opportunities.

There's no one role that's going to define an actor. There's no one audition that's going to change an actor's life. There's no one casting director that can make or break a career. You're not going to be right for all the roles you go out on and if you let go of the result, it liberates you to make it only about the work, which is the one element as an actor that you have control of— the work. Everything else is out of your hands.

Me: What should actors never do in the room with you or just in general? What should they never do, and that you have seen them do?

Mark: I assume every actor needs the job or they wouldn't be there. What you don't want to bring into the room is that need for the job resonating or emanating from you. That's not attractive. I just want an actor who is there to do the work and not there to please me. I don't need to hear how much you relate to the characters. There's just a vibe that comes off an actor that needs the work and that makes me a little uncomfortable. I want an actor prepared. I don't want excuses. I've had actors say they just got the material. I make the material available days in advance. I don't want to hear an excuse or an apology. I have hired at least three actors for series regular roles that have only had the material for ten minutes because we switched the roles we wanted them to look at. They were able to make it work because they came in and they made bold, strong choices.

Every actor is capable of that. No excuses. Whether you've had a scene for ten days or ten minutes, I want to see a connection to the material. I want to see something. I understand that actors work long hours and have crazy, ridiculous jobs, and I totally respect that. When you come in that room, you have to be an actor, not somebody apologizing for not getting material.

When actors say to me they've never seen the show, my feeling is we've been on fifty years. You've had ample opportunity to watch it. Watch an episode before you come in. In fact I would say to any actor if you get the opportunity to read for any show that's on the air, at least watch an episode on your computer, on your iPhone, on the television, so you know the show you're going in for.

There's no reason not to be familiar with the tone and the sensibility of the show. It's different with pilots and movies where there's no previous episode. Do a little homework. It's a business. Know what you're going in for. Those are basics but sometimes actors forget that.

I'll sometimes ask an actor if they have any questions. By that, I mean if they have any questions about the work that are specific to the material that might help. Don't ask a question just for the sake asking. If you have no questions, it's okay to say no I've made some choices. I've had a few actors say, when I've asked do you have any questions, "Yes, when are the callbacks?" When that's the question they ask me, I immediately think, "I wouldn't worry about it if I were you."

Just use your common sense. Be a professional. Most actors are. I've had nothing but really lovely experiences through the years with actors. I only mention these scenarios because they're more aberrations than the norm. It's a very competitive business and you're there because you have the possibility of getting a job. Make it your chance to bring the scene to life.

Me: Going to the fact that there are so many actors, do you look at every submission?

Mark: I look at every submission. If I don't look at every submission, I'm not doing my job.

Me: How many of the submissions do you look at that are from agencies as opposed to direct submissions?

Mark:	The submissions that I get for a specific role are from the agents and managers, people that I have the relationships with. I get unsolicited submissions on a weekly basis from actors. I look at every single photo and resumé that comes in. You never know…
Me:	How do you have time for a personal life? (Laughing)?
Mark:	My job is my job and at the end of the day, I'm able to go and have my life. Although when I'm watching a movie or television show, as much as I enjoy it, I'm also doing my job because I'm always looking for talent. Actors who are unsolicited, actors without agents and managers can get auditions, but it's very difficult to build a career without representation just because of the sheer numbers.
Me:	What's the best advice you can give an actor just starting out whether they're young or advanced in age?
Mark:	Do it because you love it. Don't do it for the fame. Don't do it for the "fifteen minutes." Do it because you love the craft of acting and it's in your heart and soul. It's the most difficult profession there is that I'm aware of. Maybe that and being a musician or an artist. If you don't do it for the right reasons, you'll be miserable. If you love acting and it's in your blood, that's what will be the element that will sustain you through the highs and the low of this business.
Me:	Do you open up the roles that you put out on breakdowns to all the agencies?
Mark:	If I put a role on breakdown, it goes out to everybody. There are relationships I've developed in the business based on trust and taste. There are agencies that have incredible clients. Obviously, there are agencies that I will be excited about seeing their submissions. There's a reason they are established agencies. They represent

a certain caliber of actor, but I'm not doing my job if I am not open to all the agencies.

I put out a breakdown for a twenty-five year old female about four months ago, and within three days I had fifteen hundred submissions.

Me: Typically how long do you put out a breakdown before you actually start the casting process?

Mark: It depends. Ideally I like to have a lot of lead to me where I put it out weeks before hand so that I have the time to go through all the submissions and set up the auditions. But the truth of the matter is, sometimes a role will come up at the last minute. I've been in a situation where I've had literally three days' notice and I've had to put out a breakdown and read hundreds of actors within those three days. I had another situation where I auditioned three hundred actresses in four days.

I had another role that was a one to two month recurring role, and fourteen hundred submissions came in. If an actor knows that nine hundred to fifteen hundred actors are usually submitted for every role, they have to understand they're not going to get in for every role that they think they're right for.

Me: Let's say you decided not to call someone in just based on a submission. Have you ever had an experience where the agent would call to pitch a particular actor and has convinced you to see that actor, and had then that actor gotten the role?

Mark: I've had situations where an agent has pitched somebody that I didn't necessarily want to bring in at first and ended up being the person that booked the role. I've also had the reverse where an agent had pitched someone for a role and they came in but they were not what I was looking for. I'm not this fortress of solitude. It's a collaborative business. I have relationships with the agents and managers who I respect and trust. If I'm not listening, I'm not doing my job. I'm not here to say no. I'm here to say yes. Somebody once said to me, you have such a tough job because you say no to so many people. I've never looked at it that way. I say yes to so many people.

Me: Have you had any surprises?

Mark: Best surprise is when somebody that I've never met before comes into the room and from the moment they walk in, I feel like I'm with somebody really interesting and they actually get the role, and it becomes even bigger than I imagined. That happens a lot, fortunately, or I wouldn't be here and we wouldn't be as successful. Those are the things that give me the ultimate satisfaction. Those moments where I feel I'm in the presence of, not only the person that's going to get the role, but somebody that I'm excited to cast in the role. Those are the moments a casting director lives for.

Me: I don't think that actors really understand what a difficult job you have because you do have to narrow it down and you do genuinely care about everybody who comes in this room.

Mark: There's a lot of pressure in casting. I don't think actors are always aware that we're under a lot of pressure. We might be working on three or four roles at once, multiple projects at once. We have to please producers, writers, and audition actors. We're getting swamped by phone calls, by agents, managers pitching. Basically, we're in the middle of a hurricane, and so I think an actor can sometimes feel like they walk in the room and they're just a commodity. I try to be warm to every actor, but I'm not there to be your friend. I'm there to cast a role.

           What I should always be aware of in casting is that no matter how stressful my day, I need to be polite and present and allow the actor the opportunity to do good work. In a given day, I'm reading thirty, forty people. I've had days where I've auditioned eighty actors in a day. Actors have to understand that the bottom line is we're looking to hire somebody. I'm not looking to say no. If the actor understands when they walk in the room that I want to hire them, that's a very liberating place to come from. I'm not looking to reject you, I'm looking to hire you. You may be the exact the answer to my problem.

If you do good work, whether you get called back or not, you will be remembered. The best thing an actor can do is do good work. Karmically, that stays in a casting director's consciousness. It might not be for that role. It might not even be for that show, but they'll be remembered, and you'll start to build a relationship with that particular casting director.

Relationships don't come from cocktail parties or schmoozing. Relationships come from going into the room and doing good work. You do that, you've already developed a good relationship with the casting director.

Scott David,
Casting Director, Criminal Minds

Scott is currently the casting director for the hit show, *Criminal Minds*, which is stating its ninth season on CBS. He's been a casting director since his work on the hit show, *Nash Bridges*, and has since worked on numerous projects including Dean Devlin's *Leverage*.

Scott also casts numerous independent feature films every year, and in July 2012, he began *The Actors Link*, which is considered to be one of the top workshops in Hollywood, giving actors the opportunity to work on material for casting directors, agents, and managers.

Me: With the advent of Internet casting technology, do you still do general meetings with actors, or are they a thing of the past?

Scott: I think generals will always be around. It's just for me, I always like meeting new people. If an agent or manager finds something interesting about somebody that they've met that they want me to meet, I will gladly sit down with that person for five or ten minutes. Sometimes it swings into one or two or three or four hours. I'm always open to amending my schedule.

Me: When it turns into two, three, four hours, what is it about that person that you say, "Wow I've got to know this person more?"

Scott: It's kind of that elusive "it" factor, and it depends on how friendly the person is, how friendly I'm feeling and it's the same as making a bond as friend. Sometimes the conversations will be more open to exploring different lives and where they've gone in the history of their career, what they're doing with their career...

Me: Do you ever see newcomers or do you only look at people with credits?

Scott: Oh no, I always like to find newcomers. I'm always exploring the people that have no credits or very few credits or just getting into the business and watching them grow and seeing where they go with their careers.

Me: How many actors do you actually see for, let's say, a guest star or co-star role as opposed to how many actors are submitted?

Scott: Actually, submissions depend on the type of role, the type of character that I'm looking for. If I put out a breakdown for a certain character— sometimes I don't because I have them in my inventory in my office, in my files— but typically speaking, anywhere from 500 to 2,000 people are submitted per role and the people that I would audition and actually view, anywhere from only one to maybe ten people.

Me: That's a pretty low number considering how many are submitted.

Scott: Yes.

Me: Do you have your favorite agencies that you go to for these positions always or do you try to include people from—

Scott: Everybody's included in the breakdowns. When I'm specifically looking for something and I know that an agency represents a certain type of character or a certain class of character, or ethnicity, or something very specific, if I feel they're known for representing more mature people versus youthful people, I would look to certain agents and agencies for those types of characters.

Typically speaking, yes, we all have our favorites in the business, people that we like to do business with, people that are receptive to phone calls and our needs, as well as being receptive to their needs and their pitches. You make relationships and utilize them when you need to.

Me: When you're casting a role and you've got your breakdowns out and you've chosen maybe your one or ten people, what should actors never do when they come into the room with you?

Scott: Well I always try to stress what they <u>should</u> do versus what they should never do.

             If they just do what I call these two things, they're usually pretty safe. One is to be prepared, and the other is to be appropriate. If they just concentrate on those two general subject matters and forget about all the negativity, those two things will put them in a better space.

             That's kind of how I always phrase that and that's something that I've kind of preached for a long time.

Me: Can you briefly walk us through the casting process from breakdown to pre-reads to screen tests, because I think a lot of people starting out really don't understand the length of this process?

Scott: For a pilot or for a regular TV show?

Me: Either for a pilot or for a series regular?

Scott: Well for a series regular you start a search when you get a pilot and you have discussions with the studios, network, and the producers and you figure out what type of character you're looking for: age range, potential ethnicity, type, look, that type of stuff. Then you put out a breakdown and then hundreds upon hundreds upon hundreds upon hundreds of people submit, and then you start filtering through, as a casting director, who you want to read, who you want to meet, who is already seasoned and will go straight to the producers and not need to have a pre-read. Most of the time pre-reads are done in pilots for more youthful people because they don't have a body of work yet so you're really looking to find and search out these people that potentially could be brought to the producers and then go further. As people age and get more credits, and they've done more things, they go straight to producers. If the producers like them, then they might go on to a studio test or network test and then they might get the job. You never know, but it's a long involved process, usually, and it's fun and happens quite a few times. (Laughing)

Me: Now how much say do you as a casting director actually get in who gets a role, or who's considered for a role, or who's in?

Scott: Episodically as the casting director I have 100% control because I'm the one that's making the first decision of who's going to be coming in the room.

If you look at it from that angle, I've already chosen because one out of those ten are going to get the job. So I have complete control. Once we go into the room and the director and the producer and myself are there, we meet the people and then we decide as a team at the end who we like. Sometimes there's a little bit more of a discussion and we hash it out, and either see more people if we're not all in agreement, or we pick the person after we've discussed it. In my particular situation, it's a team effort.

Me: You've also cast *Leverage*. You've been on some pretty big TV shows.

Scott: I did *Leverage* in the first two seasons, but that's been a few years back.

Me: Since you also cast films, can you tell us the difference between casting for films as opposed to casting for episodic television?

Scott: The process and the people— and I'm talking about independent films, because I do a lot of independent films— usually the producers and directors are a little bit more novice. Some have done some things, some need a lot of education in the casting process because if they've done short films, or this or that or the other, they've used friends and stuff like that. Introducing them to the casting process and all headaches and all the nightmares of agents and managers and who will come in and who won't come in and how many people we need to see and who would be an offer… just that whole education is really exciting for me to teach to new people. (Laughing) That whole process is really fun. Sometimes it's painstaking, but it's really really fun.

                Then there are other people that have done films before and are much more seasoned on the processes and a little bit more mainstreamed, and we know we're going to see this many people, we know we're going to look for this character for a few days and we're going to make an offer, and everybody's on the same page.

                Typically speaking, for some, the process is not under so much pressure. You have a little bit more time. Usually you have four weeks to two months to cast a film, whereas in episodic television you have eight days or less, sometimes, to cast twenty roles. And sometimes in a film you're only casting ten roles and you have two months. The process is a little bit slower. The search is a little bit more diverse, and you have just a little bit more time to work with

	the director and see what his or her vision is more specifically for the characters.

Me: What in your opinion would hold actors back from getting work in the industry?

Scott: Holding them back… I think that's always a personal thing for an actor. Sometimes it's a confidence level. Sometimes it's strictly business level, if they have the proper representation to get them into rooms. Sometimes it's a skill level, they're not really ready yet— they have to be in classes. Other times, it's a complete, I hate to say it, but a looks level and an age level, what you look like and what your age is. It's a variety of things.

Me: What's the biggest challenge in what you do?

Scott: The biggest challenge is being on the front line. We're the messenger, quite often, and the mediator between producers and directors and agents and managers and actors. Being on that front line and hearing the truths and hearing the b.s., and hearing all that kind of stuff is the biggest challenge, and then having to communicate it delicately or bluntly to the directors and producers of the project. I would say the biggest challenge is finding that balance of being in the middle.

Being the middle man, and we're the middlemen, the conduit to the talent and the production.

Me: So I imagine that position is fairly stressful because you have a vision of what the role should be, as well.

Scott: Yes. I can personally give you an example without names, of course.

A director asks you to look for an A-List star for a very

low budget movie, and I'm talking an A-List star I know.

Well, who's directing? What's the budget, how much are they going to get paid, what are the elements of the project?

No, they're not going to do that project. I know. I know factually. Is there any relationship there? No. They completely say nope, they're not available, or no, they're not interested in doing a small film like that.

Then you have to go back to the producer or the director and tell them this A-List star is not interested in their project. As a casting director who's done it a million times, you already pre-know that. Yes, there is that one-in-a-million chance that the [A-Lister] might say yes. I don't deny anybody the opportunity of asking because all they're going to say is yes or no.

The reps unleash the meanness on the casting director and the casting director has to delicately tell the producer and director that, no, they didn't respond to your material, or no, they're not interested in doing a low budget film right now. You have to tell them that kind of stuff and you just have to tell them delicately. I'm in the process of doing that with a few people right now.

(Laughing) I'm looking for an email this morning saying, "Are you fucking kidding me?" (Laughing) It was sent last night at midnight.

Me: Good luck with that.

Scott: Ha. Yes. Sometimes directors, especially newcomers, are delusional that they think they might be able to get these stars. They're not going to get them. They're just not.

93

Me:	Would that be one of your biggest pet peeves or do you have a bigger one?
Scott:	Oh, that's a pet peeve thing on the production/ directing side, but some actors... I just go back to be appropriate and be prepared.
Me:	What's the best advice you can give to actors just starting out?
Scott:	Well, it's a two-fold thing. Figuring out your master plan, figuring out your budget and then jumping into studying— acting classes and doing casting director workshops— so that you can get yourself in front of different casting directors and start to formulate relationships with assistants, associates, and casting directors.
	You've really got to plan, and get some guidance and consultation in what you're going to do with your career, because if the newbie is coming out of college, they have no idea what goes in on in actual Hollywood because none of the colleges prepare them for that. They do a lot of scene study, a lot of theater work, and then they're thrown into the jungle of Hollywood and they don't know what to do. I meet all these kinds of people, oftentimes, in workshops that I do, and then try to guide them and help them with the things that give them tools to grow in their career.
Me:	Can actors do something more proactive about their careers for people like you to see them more if they don't have an agent or a manager or someone submitting on their behalf?
Scott:	I own a workshop, *The Actors Link* in Hollywood. It's about getting in front of agents, managers, and casting directors, and figuring out how you're going to start relationships. Not hounding the casting director, but

showing them your work and getting into showcases, getting into theater, getting into group acting things where you put on performances, there's all kinds of stuff. Anything that you can do that hopefully somebody will come and see it.

* * *

Scott is known among actors and industry pros for his positive and upbeat, fun-loving nature, and it shows in his work and in his workshop, **The Actors Link***, from which he has been known to call in actors for auditions. For workshop information, visit* **www.ActorsLinkLA.com.**

Renita Gale Swaekauski,
Casting Director, Commercials & Film

I'm thrilled to have interviewed Renita because she is not only one of the top commercial casting directors in town, she is also one of my dearest friends. Having met on a party plane going to Sundance in 1999, we ended up sitting next to each other and hit it off immediately. Renita is a heart-centered and positive professional, who not only lives from that place, but strives to inspire others, as well.

At the time we met, she was not yet a casting director, so I have watched her start and grow her company, Renita Casting, into one of the busiest and most respected offices. She is also know for casting the acclaimed film, *Spun*, starring Jason Schwartzman, Mickey Rourke, Mena Suvari and the late Brittany Murphy.

Plus, Renita is an accomplished actor and voice-over artist, having such notable reoccurring work as one of Pandora's most-used announcers.

Me: How and why did you get into casting?

Renita: I grew up an actor. I'm an actor through and through, and so when I first made my foray into the entertainment industry it was as a production manager, line producer, and producer back in Boston. Because Boston's film community was so small, when I was producing, production managing and line producing, I also had the opportunity to take on other jobs, not for more money but for more fun, and I would always ask if I could participate with the actors. I would do my job and I would do whatever it took to get to participate with the actors, and so I'd end up casting the movies that I would work on or be involved in it just for the fun of it.

When I moved to LA, the same thing started to happen where I was, well, there one instance in particular where I was production managing an industrial, and the producer told me he had this much money for hiring the casting director, and I said to him, "Well, if I get my regular production manager job done, would you mind if I just keep the casting money, and I'll do the casting job, too?" He said, "I don't care, just get it done however you want to do it." I said, "Great."

I did that, and it was an all-kids casting. It was a Mattel job, and the day after the Mattel job, I went to meet with a producer on the set of a Disney job about more production work. There was a kid on the set of the Disney job that we had just used in the Mattel job, right? I looked over and I'm like, oh, I just cast that kid in this Mattel thing we did the other day. Though I was handing the producer a resumé full of production experience, he associated me with casting.

A couple of months later, this producer called me out of the blue. He was actually production managing a big music video for a director who was just coming on the scene at the time named Dave Myers, who has gone on to become one of the most successful, well-known music video and commercial directors in the industry. Dave Myers at the time had just gotten on the map doing a music video for a little artist named Kid Rock. Dave's regular casting director was out of town because it was July 4th weekend, 1999. The town was shut up tight, and they needed to start casting, like, now! This production manager said, "Hey I know somebody," and he called me up, and he said, "Hey listen, are you available to start casting a music video right now if we hire you? Send over your resume." I said, "Well, yeah, I'm available," because that's one thing I learned in my career is you never say no, you say, yes, and then you figure it out later. (Laughter).

I said, "Well, yeah, I'm available, but my resumé has no casting on it." He said, "That's okay. I've already vouched for you. Just send it over." I sent over my resumé and he called me twenty minutes later. He said, "You're on. You got the job." That was a music video for Def Leppard for the song *Goodbye*, so the very first job of my career was *Goodbye*.

Then to make it even more fantastic, it just so happened that a very good friend of mine was a very successful actress who was working a lot. She was over at my house when the call came for the job, and so I had no time to turn this job around to cast it. As I was looking for my leading lady in the music video, I turned to her, and I was like, "Would you ever want to do a music video?" She said, "Yeah, it sounds like fun."

I managed to get this up-and-coming notable actress in this music video. Not only did I do street casting for Dave and put together this massive task, but I ended up getting a notable actress in the lead so I was just on the map. I then became known as the independent film girl who could find anyone for your project.

Me: You cast Indie films, you cast commercials, you cast music videos… what has been the primary thing that you cast over the years, like the main bread and butter stuff?

Renita: Well, the main bread and butter stuff is definitely general market commercials, but if I go back a little bit I always enjoy mentioning the feature film, *Spun*, because it's the one notable feature I've done so far in my career, and it was just an extraordinary and rewarding experience.

Me: The commercial world has changed quite a bit in the last couple of years, right? A lot of stuff is non-union now. Is that correct?

Renita: Yes, it is.

Me: How has that affected the quality of the talent that
             comes in, now that a lot of stuff is non-union?

Renita: This has been a topic of much discussion as not just a
             casting director, but because I'm an actor as well. As
             an actor, you just want a work, and you want to be
             paid well for your work, and the better you get and
             the more well respected, the more you can garner for
             your talent. But as an actor, you just want to work. As
             a casting director, I want the best-possible talent even
             when I don't have as much money as I wish I had to
             offer them. What started to happen is, whereas a few
             years ago if someone came to you with a non-union
             job, the expectations were managed accordingly.

             That's not the case anymore. They expect union-
             quality performance and selection for non-union. The
             catch is, and this is where it gets a little bit tricky, is
             because the trend has been going this way for so long,
             a lot of actors have started either not going union or
             going financial core.

Me: Now that a lot of stuff is going non-union, and
             the talent expectation is the same as union, for the
             newcomer actor, for the people just out of school or
             people who are deciding they finally want to pursue
             their dreams at the age of forty, or whatever it may
             be— and some people give up their careers as a
             lawyer or a doctor— what do they need to expect in
             the positive sense and negative sense with all this
             abundance of non-union work?

Renita: Wow, I'm the "dreams come true" lady, right? I always
             want to speak from "anything you want is possible,
             and you can not only have a successful acting career,
             but you can have a lucrative one." I have to be honest,
             I think it's a tenuous time. I think that coming out of
             this phase, there will eventually be an upturn again
             because if so many producers continue to do non-
             union work, more and more actors are going to need

to and want to be able to do it, but it's going to water down the payday. More and more actors are going to be doing more work, but they're not going to be able to pay their bills and be a working actor the way the actors of even five years ago could by doing a couple commercials a year.

For the time being, unfortunately, the commercial acting world is going to be a volume-based business. It is frustrating.

Me: It's different then what it used to be like, right? It used to be that you could do a couple of national commercials and get paid on the backend, but residuals have gone by the wayside now because of non-union stuff. Isn't that correct?

Renita: Yes, exactly, and because of this ever-evolving medium called new media and Internet. We just watched *House of Cards* on Netflix, this amazing television series produced by and for Netflix. If you are watching advertising, you're dealing with Internet only advertising. A spot produced exclusively for the Internet is produced at 350% of sales, meaning an actor makes just over $1800 for either a year or 21 months, and it's one year of use for Internet only.

If you look at that where, if an actor had a spot, one per year on a national network, he could've bought a house and a car. An actor, now, does a spot that runs for a year on the Internet and makes, if they're lucky, $1800.

The only other thing I'll say is, at some point if … I hope that it'll be longer, maybe forever, before television and film will be impacted. I think that actors will still have the opportunity to make better money, commanding union rates for film and television and residuals in that way, but even residuals, they are getting watered down because of that new media.

Commercially, I think the only thing we can hope for is if enough actors, if enough companies, continue to produce non-union product, at some point you're going to have the same situation of competition where actors will be able to then demand higher rates for non-union work, because the talented ones can start commanding more rates

Me: It's a tough entry right now for the commercial. How, then, can actors be more proactive and productive in their careers?

Renita: One thing that I've been noticing— and I'm a big fan of considering the evolution of media— is creating original content. Actors getting together with other creative individuals who like to direct, to produce, who shoot and creating one series, creating original content that people could then purchased and picked up for Internet and new media outlets— because Hulu and Netflix and Amazon are not only producing their own content, but they're also going to be buying content! Because that is the future. We will be self-programming our entertainment in its entirety very soon.

Me: This is so different from when you and I started out, where people who wanted to be actors were only actors because of the theater and then went on to some TV or commercials, but now it doesn't seem like that's the case— that you could only be an actor now. It seems like you have to be a writer or a producer or a director or something else and actually not just call yourself that. You actually produce something and put it online. Would you agree with that? And how does that then change the business of acting?

Renita: Not too long ago there was this conversation community-wide about how you don't want to confuse people. You just want to be one thing. I'm an actor. I'm a producer. I'm a casting director. Even me, right? I'm a casting director. I'm a voice-over actor. I'm a producer. And nobody blinks anymore. In fact, when you're working on a project… we're casting a short film right now… and the director as we're discussing actors will come back and say, "I couldn't find any video of him online. I couldn't find enough video of her online. Why isn't there more content of her online?" In the old days, if someone had a demo reel, that was the most you could expect. Now, if you can't Google them and pull their name up on at least five YouTube clips, they can't possibly be a legitimately working actor.

I think that actors need to be doing this and nobody thinks twice anymore of an actor saying, "I act, I produce, I direct, I write, and this is the show I just did, five of these webisodes…"

Me: It's amazing how it changed that way in the five, ten years, with the advent of YouTube and Hulu and IndieGoGo and Funny or Die. If actors have to be producing their own content, how does that change what you do as a casting director? Because you're not necessarily going to have the budget for these kinds of things, but if more and more control is going that way, how do you stay on top of the game?

Renita: It's interesting because this is a conversation that Alex and I are perpetually having with ourselves and with other people— with technology changing. The part that will never go away is the need for direction, at least I hope it won't. When we audition actors, the reason that we do it and submit the auditions to the client is because we talk to the client. We're experts in the field. We know how to set up a scene, and we know how to adjust the performance to give the actor a chance of getting the role. Even if they're off the mark or on the mark, even if they're way too big, you can get them to go smaller, and so on.

That's the part of the job that I don't think is going anywhere any time soon. I think the way that we're rolling with the times is we've started looking at alternative ways to provide the client with what they need within their budget, while taking down time and expense. One of the ways is we're now using technology for our benefit. In other words, instead of holding first round auditions, we're having actors self submit their first round audition by video, and then we're culling through those, and then we're presenting the favorites.

I did a job a couple of years ago that was completely auditioned, called-back and shot entirely over iChat!

I think studios will always exist. Actors will always need to come in for a callback, or maybe not always, but often. I think the thing that is going to change, and thus radically slash budgets and make things more affordable, is that we can keep up with the times and present new, innovative ways to show the client what they're looking for using current technology where actors never need to leave their house to audition.

Me: Do you think that would probably be more prevalent in the commercial casting processes because commercial is such a high-volume, fast turnaround, and then the clients don't have to fly anywhere? Do you think that's going to happen in the commercial industry first and do you think it's going to be widespread?

Renita: I think commercially for sure, but what's interesting is if you look at the theatrical world, actors have been putting themselves on tape for decades. Actors have been self-submitting their original audition a lot longer than commercial actors have. I think that commercial, in a way, is just finally catching up. Except we're doing it with the top technology. You know, everything's expected to be yesterday and five minutes ago, and cheaper in an instant.

Me: Can you tell me your biggest pet peeve as a casting director?

Renita: I'll give it to you in a couple layers. When an actor does not have a proper headshot, first of all, because if they do not take their career seriously enough to seek out a great headshot photographer, get a good photo, and get it up online, they're not serious about acting. That's the first thing.

To go hand-in-hand with that, an actor who comes in not looking like their headshot drives me crazy because it wastes everybody's time. Contrary to popular belief where clients think that all the actors live in my living room and I know them all personally and I know what they looked like yesterday (Laughing)— their agents don't even know what they looked like yesterday. If an actor isn't keeping their headshots current and then comes in ten pounds heavier, twenty pounds thinner, forty years older. (Laughter)

Here's the thing. I say this to actors all time. Save your favorite, beautiful, arty, well hair-brushed, perfectly lit—well, headshots should be perfectly lit—but save the best pictures of you... for Facebook. You want your headshots to look like you. We all know how that works. We all understand that makeup and lighting makes a difference, but my goodness, when people come in looking nothing like their photos, I wonder what universe they think they're playing in. Are people just going to go, "She's twenty years older than the photo she submitted for that twenty-two year old, part but gosh, she was just so good?" It's never going to happen! Especially with commercials, you're dealing with well-researched, painstakingly-researched demographics.

Me:	Then conversely, what do you love what actors do and wish they would do more of?
Renita:	I want to speak to something specifically, which is that I've been looking a lot at myself lately, and continuing with my own investigation about what makes the business successful, what makes the person successful. One thing is that people do business with people they trust and feel like they have something in common with.

One of the most common quibbles for actors—because of the nature of the "business dynamic" is—they regard themselves as the seller and the casting directors, agents, directors, producers, production companies as it's a buyer. While that's true, it's a very disempowering conversation whereas I think one of the greatest things that an actor can do is regard their casting director as their partner, ally, and compatriot. We *need* them to be the one we've been dreaming of seeing, as much as *they* need *us* to see them as the one we've been dreaming of.

When an actor enters the room in partnership—and one of the things that indicates partnership is that they're present, they listen, they can really hear when you're giving them directions… They've come prepared. They have you as an equal. They don't have you above them. They don't have you below them. They come in going, "Let's do the work together."

One bit of coaching I give actors, when I do my personal coaching with them, is I get them present to the difference in the way they feel when they walk onto set. They've already been hired for the job, versus they walk into a room for an audition to get the job. Then I get them present to the fact that the only distinction is their way of thinking about it. There's a declaration called "You have the job." If they can just get that owning the space of "peace and fulfillment and partnership" exits when they go to set already having been hired, it can exist all through their acting process. It makes our job so much easier because we don't have to deal with people being weird.

If we can give you a direction and you hear it, then you get that we're giving you the direction not to mess you up. Because who would ever do that? But we give you the direction to have you win and because we know exactly what we're looking for. It's like if every time a production company calls me, or an Ad agency calls me to hire me for casting, if I got all weird, they'd never hire me. But I know we're here to do a job together, and they rely on me for my expertise and I rely on them for theirs. Together, we produce great stuff.

Me: What is your biggest challenge in what you do as casting director?

Renita: At this point, I would say it goes back to your question about the changing industry. At this moment, quite honestly, our business has become a volume-based business as well. People have smaller budgets, less per day rate, and they want it quicker and better. First rule of producing: do you want it good, do you want it fast, do you want it cheap? Pick two.

We really love it when a producer calls us and says, "I need it cheap, and I need it good so here's two weeks to do it" or "I need it fast and I need it good. Here's your full rate. We need it top notch." When they know they're not paying full rate, they're still going to get a great job, but you know, maybe they're not going to have certain little perks, or things at callbacks we would normally put in our full-rate jobs.

When expectations are in line with expenditures, it makes our life easy, but one of the things that we've been encountering is, just like actors— we also may not work for weeks or months at a time. No so much anymore, but when we would do a job, that job could pay the bills for months, just like an actor. Now we're needing to do two and three jobs to make the same amount of income we used to make from one job. Or they used to have two callbacks, and now they've got one callback for the same number of people in the cast. We're doing more. They're paying less, but they want the same quality, if not better.

Me: What is the best advice you can give to someone just starting out?

Renita: I'll share this, and if you want to include it please feel free. It's s one of my favorite quotes by Howard Thurman: "Don't ask what the world needs, ask what makes you come alive and go do it because what the world needs is people who have come alive." It really embodies everything I stand for.

           If this is truly your passion, if acting makes you come alive, go do it. Just don't ever need for it to make you money. If you're someone going into it as a second career, you've made your money as a doctor, you built your law practice, you won the lottery, your uncle died and left you a lot of money and you can afford to be a full-time actor, train, and give it everything you've got to succeed and you keep going, I promise you, you will make money and you will succeed. It may take ten years, but you will succeed if you can continue and you train because you'll become a master. Never need what you love to make you money. That is a very dangerous recipe.

           If you don't have the good fortune of having built your law practice or won the lottery or had your uncle leave you money, and you're someone who actually needs to live and pay the bills and pursue your passion, then you need to create a life that sustains all of that. You need to find a context that empowers you around that. In other words, if you have a full time job as a nanny because you also love doing that, but your real passion is acting, both can coexist. You just have to make it work. In other words, the money, and the freedom you get from the money you earn being a nanny, will create the stage for you to go on auditions and take classes and perform and produce your own content. Then, hopefully, some day you won't need the nanny job anymore.

That's my greatest bit of advice. At the same time, the other side of it is, a lot of the people who are truly successful at anything are people that give their heart and soul, who are willing to live with four people in a one-bedroom apartment and work a night job and literally live a certain type of life to pursue their art, to pursue their craft. I'm not saying that one is better than the other at all. If that's really what it means for you, and I don't mean to be pessimistic, because people succeed all the time. There's money to be made. There's success to be had, but I feel strongly that it can only come out of going at life from doing what makes you come alive, not going at it because you need to make money.

* * *

Renita truly lives to inspire in everything she does. She has created a **Transformational Declaration CD** *for Actors, available on her website,* **www.RenitaCasting.com,** *to help actors visualize their success and transform their careers. She also hosts a podcast and privately coaches actors.*

The Teachers

Scott Sedita,
Scott Sedita Acting Studios

Scott Sedita is one of LA's master teachers. Known for his on-camera film & TV classes, he is also considered the top teacher for comedy offering classes like Sitcom Character & Technique, and his Advanced Sitcom class.

Scott offers a unique perspective that most other instructors don't, not just because he started out as an actor, but because he was a successful agent in New York City, having helped launch the careers of Courtney Cox and Matt LeBlanc. He then became a top casting director in Los Angeles, working for the legendary Danny Goldman, when he discovered his gift for teaching.

He has also become one of the top go-to on-set coaches for numerous productions, and is the author of what is widely considered the definitive book for TV comedy acting and writing, *The Eight Characters of Comedy,* which is currently used as a textbook in over eighty colleges and universities.

Me: What do you think of new media, social media... ?

Scott: The good news is that actors have a lot more resources for self-producing. It's great idea working on a web series. Anything you can get to work on. The good part about that is that it's good to work, and work begets work.

                 The bad part about that for actors is that you've got to be careful in saying, "I just did a film." When it ends up really not being a film. It ends up being that you're someone's brother-in-law who wanted to shoot something. That's not something you necessarily would put down on your resume and hope to get an IMDb credit for. It's not a professional film.

                 It's becoming so easy for people to see work. Someone called me up and said, "Listen, I'm working on this pilot, who do you have that's funny?"

113

I said, "I have a couple of people. Let me send you someone that I think is really terrific and that would be great for you."

In the old days, the casting directors— it was easy to say, "What's his name?" "His name is John Doe." Now, today, it's, "I want to see him," and the casting director is watching something while I'm on the phone with them. They're basically checking out this person I recommended on a video. I don't know where they got the video. They're checking his personality on video. Then they say to me, "He's not good at comedy."

I know for a fact that this person is good for comedy. I know their work. Whatever video they put up from three years ago, it's not good. Just because you appear on camera, doesn't mean it's good. Actors have to be very careful on what they put out there.

Me: You've got an audition class. Is it just about getting the job? What do you do?

Scott: This is the class that I've been doing for 15 years. We have level one, level two, and then the professional class. It's designed for actors who already have foundation, who have the nuts and bolts scene study underneath them, have a foundation in their craft, in what they're going to use in order to get where they need to get emotionally.

            That's how it's basically designed. I know how to help an actor not only get stronger in their craft and teach them more technique, but also tell them how to break down an audition script. You might not even get to read the whole script. Maybe you will, but these sides that you have… you need to learn how to break those sides down quickly and efficiently so you can get excited and stay excited during this process of working on your audition.

114

I have an audition technique called WOFRAIM. What is your Want, Obstacle, the Feelings you've got to explore in the scene, the Relationship you have with the other person, the As-if— what's you're personal substitution— your Intentions— the actions you take in order to get what you want to seduce, to crush, to mock— and M is the Moment before. What are you emotionally feeling as you enter the scene and where are you as you enter the scene? Which is part of my app— I'm the first acting coach to have an app that teaches actors how to breakdown their sides.

The other thing I teach in my audition technique classes is how to bring yourself into the room and into every character. Ultimately, the way to win the room is to bring yourself into the room and how to integrate yourself into every character. It's really important.

What's happened in the last five years is that 98% of all casting directors for professional television and film have a camera in the studio now. This setup— when actors enter the room— has a reader to the right of the camera, and the camera is recording.

The class teaches how to deal with that environment that's really artificial. You have to have a fourth wall. You have to know where you are. You have to make the reader the other person. That's really difficult to be able to do.

Not only that, now you have to be very clear that you're on camera, and your angels to the camera have to be right. Turning your back on camera is not going to read, or dropping down all of sudden to pick something up— you'll be out of frame or walking off. You have to be able to deal with having a camera there.

That audition— even if it's at 5:00 in the afternoon— is going to be sent to the producer or the director of the show. They want to see that you're able to do it right for camera right away. They want to see that you can be in the moment and that you're camera-ready for your forty-five seconds as the cop or the paramedic or the receptionist or the stranger who says, "He went that way."

Me: Let's talk about the comedy class that you teach. How is that different from traditional acting classes?

Scott: It's completely different. First and foremost, what I'm trying to do is make funny actors. Right there it sets something aside. I'm just not trying to make funny people. What I teach is actual single camera and multi-camera sitcom acting, which is a very very different technique and has very different rules.

The first thing you need is to be an actor. You need to have a good foundation, not just some bold scene study. That foundation, it needs to be really really strong. What comedy does is bring a whole new dimension it. It has a whole set of rules. It's heady in a lot of ways. The technique is heady.

There are characterizations which are the *Eight Characters of Comedy*, and that's a whole separate issue. What you want to be able to do is mix your acting foundation with comedy technique and the eight characters of comedy and have them harmoniously join together. That's a process which takes time.

The good thing about the eight characters of comedy, it helps actors organically go towards a character that is inside them somewhere. It's an archetype. They have characteristics that would be closer to one of the characters than the others. If we look at comedy characters, if we look at just the queen of comedy or the queen of sitcom, Betty White, she's played two very different characters. It's really just those two characters, which is the dumb one in your own universe and the bitch man-izer.

116

Those are the two things that she's played. There's no neurotic there. There's not even the materialistic one. There's no entitlement to any of her stuff that she does. What she's known for are those two different types of characters. That's what she's been doing for, like, sixty years.

Not everybody can do all of the eight characters of comedy— maybe on stage, but not on television— where the camera is so close and the way you look and the way your essence comes through.

Me: Can anybody learn to be funny?

Scott: It's the same way can anybody learn to be an actor? Next to the acting gene, there has to be the funny gene. You have to have a sense of humor about life. You have to have a sense of humor about yourself. You have to have sense of humor *period*.

I work with so many Emmy Award winning dramatic actors, and let me tell you, it's hard. It's tough to teach them comedy, sometimes. They have to be willing to learn the rules of comedy, which, at the very basic level, is you can't change a word. Why? The words are rhythm. It's the notes in a song. You can't change the notes in the song.

Me: A third aspect to what you do is also you go to set to coach people on-set. Let's talk about that a little bit. A lot of times people think once they're on TV, they've made it, they don't need classes anymore...

Scott: Famous actors don't take class. Sure, there's always the talk about that one person who showed up in that one class. Basically, it's my experience that actors who are working— who are on a series, a regular on a TV show, or starring in some films— are not usually in class. That doesn't mean they don't coach. They still coach. They'll come to my house. They'll come to my studio. I'll come to them, their house. I do a lot of that or I'll come on to the set and work with them in their trailer.

Me: Why would they feel they would need you on a set?

Scott: They just want to be better at whatever they're working on, or go deeper dramatically, or just find the funny. I think it's great.

Me: What is the biggest challenge in what you do as a teacher?

Scott: The biggest challenge... my classes are different than, let's say, a scene study teacher. Let's say one of the top scene study teachers. They have fifty people in a class. Not everybody can work, otherwise they would be there until the next day. What I do is everyone works. Everyone has to work.

Every class, they work twice a class. That's what I'm known for because the more you work, the more you practice. Sitting in a class watching people is not ... I don't think that's a good thing. It's fine to do that and you learn from it. Watch a good movie. Watch Meryl Streep or Pacino or De Niro or Daniel Day-Lewis and watch the film once and get entertained by it. Then watch it again and just watch them do their work.

In my class, you get up and you work. Why that makes it difficult for me is because let's say I have sixteen people— I only allow sixteen people per class. That's a lot of individual attention. I have to give sixteen individual people who have their own needs, individual attention.

It's hard for me because I want to make sure everybody gets something. In my classes, it's the reason I'm successful. People feel they've left with something. They've grown. You grow faster that way.

That being said, once again, my classes are not for the

118

new actor. It would be much better for that actor to go to a scene study class or a nuts and bolts type of a class to get that type of work so they'll be ready for me. What I do is not just help with their craft, I also help them with their careers. I have a whole book about it. It's called *The Typing Game*.

Me: Let's talk about type for a minute. What do you do to help actors with type?

Scott: Fifteen years ago, I came from casting. I thought, "What an interesting thing— actors don't know who they are." I wrote a book about it, *The Eight Characters of Comedy*. Trying to find ways for actors to understand who they are or where they fit in. I do the *Typing Game* right from the very beginning. You're sitting here and the students all write adjectives about you while I talk to you. It gives you an idea of who you are. It helps you find out what type you are.

Me: What do you think is one of the biggest things that keep actors from getting— ?

Scott: Fear.

Me: Of?

Scott: Fear of failure and fear of success.

Me: Is there really a fear of success?

Scott: Yeah. I just booked a girl as a series regular. Her first fear was that it would go terrible. She would be embarrassed and humiliated in front of her agents and managers and anyone in the network. We had the screen test. She got over that.

Now she's gotten the series regular role. Everybody wants to know her. Now, she has to go on to the set— it's not so much fear of embarrassment and humiliation because she knows she's got it— it's that she has to now be as good as she was. She has to somehow be as good as she was in that screen test. Be as good as she was when she auditioned. That's where the fear of success comes in.

Me: What can you prescribe for actors to deal with the stress of the business side of the industry?

Scott: Someone who's been doing their time in the business has acclimated to the disappointment, the rejection and the success that they've had. It's always that saying, "It's better when you're older when you're successful." It is in a lot of ways it is, because you've gone through the all experiences.

           Doing the work and training, training and practice, practice and staying in the game and roughing it out during the hard times gives you the backbone, gives you the work ethic.

Me: For people just starting out, what would you suggest that they really focus on?

Scott: Training. If they can get behind their craft, if they can really learn how to prepare for their work, the more confident they will feel. They'll have more confident foundation inside of them to deal with what's going to happen next that next level. They'll have a little more of that feeling of, "I've been through this. I understand. I know. I'm ready." As opposed to "What the hell?"

Me: What should actors never do out there?

Scott: They shouldn't come to LA and not train and only take casting director workshops. They shouldn't come to LA and say, "I have $2,000 worth of money for training," and not do any training, but just to agent-manager showcases, casting director workshop. You better be one freaking, incredible, instinctual actor.

When we become adults, we second-guess. We bring in a bunch of baggage that these young kids and teen and young adults don't have, necessarily, about the business. If you want to be an actor, in order to be the best actor, you've got to train.

Me: What do you think is the secret to longevity in this industry?

Scott: The work. It always has to be about the work and the enjoyment of doing the work. That's really the bottom line. You have to be a lifer. You have to believe, "This is what I do." You also have to change as you go along. You have to go, "Okay, now I'm thirty. Okay, now I'm forty." You change. You have to know what makes it different for you, what's different in your career.

Me: What do you love about actors?

Scott: I love their creativity, the artistry of acting, their need to want to pretend and have fun and the fact that I'm able to help them. I like that. Somehow I have a good record of being able to help an actor. I get satisfied by that.

Me: Can you tell me about your app?

Scott: The app is based on my WOFRAIM which is my acronym for script analysis technique. It helps you break down your audition sides.

It also has a bunch of tongue twisters, and stuff that actors need for every audition. It has a bunch of intentions— an intention wheel that is used on the app— It has over a hundred intentions, fifty of them will give you what the intention means in order to be able to make the other person feel a certain way. There's a practice script. There are also my auditions steps.

It also keeps track of your auditions: What was I wearing? What did the casting director say to me? Where I went... all the details of your audition.

You now also can sync all your information to your iPhone iCalendar. You can keep track of it that way. There are also bonuses coming your way on it. It's only $9.99 on iTunes for iPhone and iPad at this time.

Me: You have another book coming up?

Scott: I'm doing my second edition of the *Eight Characters of Comedy,* which is going to be very exciting. I believe it will be done by the end of the year. I feel like I have personally learned more about comedy as I've been teaching it the last few years. I already saw the reemergence of comedy coming before it happened.

It was *Modern Family* that brought comedy back. I was sitting back there going, "This is starting to happen. Comedy is coming back."

Me: Now you've got show like the *New Girl,* which is spectacular. You've got so many great sitcoms...

Scott: Absolutely. A lot of single camera. Chuck Lorre is the king. He had *Two and a Half Men* all through this. Now he has *Big Bang Theory, Mike and Molly.* He's going to have a new TV show, too.

Me: Whitney Cummings has two shows...

Scott: She does. Comedy, it's time for it to come back. I can trace you the death of comedy and the reemergence since the '80s. The fact is that at the end of the '70s, sitcoms were dead. It was the *Cosby Show* that brought sitcoms back. Then towards the end of the '80s, comedy was dead. It was *Seinfeld* and *Friends* and *Sex in the City* and those shows into the '90s that brought comedy back.

Modern Family brought the single-camera comedy back. Chuck Lorre— I don't know him, but he kept in the game with multi-camera. Those multi-camera comedies are better for syndication. They're cheaper and better. Any actor would rather be on a multi-camera comedy any day than a single-camera comedy. The schedule is amazing.

Me: How so?

Scott: You're only going to be there for a certain amount of time. The hours are almost nine to five until the taping day. With a single-camera comedy, you're around town. You can be on a set. It's film. There's a lot. There's one camera. There's a lot to do.

Me: Do you like being known as the King of Comedy Makers?

Scott: I'd like to be known as the King of Comedy (laughs). I don't care. I'd like to be known as whatever. I'm going to Russia to do a comedy there. I'm now in the works with China to do comedy there.

* * *

Scott's amazing audition app is available for iPhone and iPad, and his best-selling books are available on Amazon.com. For more information about his classes, books, and blog visit
www.ScottSeditaActing.com

Anthony Meindl,
Anthony Meindl's Actor Workshop

Anthony Meindl started teaching in 2000, and has recently been voted number one acting school in Los Angels by Backstage. Anthony Meindl's Actor Workshop now boasts schools in New York, Vancouver, London, Sydney, and Melbourne, with more locations on the horizon.

Anthony teaches a non-method way of acting, and he incorporates his roots as Yoga practitioner, and uses mind-body techniques to get an actor to the organic level, the realness.

He is also an acclaimed writer and director, and authored the best-selling book, "At Left Brain Turn Right."

Me: You're creating quite the empire. (Laughs) And you're known as the best school in, not just this town, but, it seems, *every* town. (Laughs) Just reading the reviews of your best-seller, "Left Turn at Right Brain," and being voted number one school— that's really quite impressive.

Anthony: I don't really know what to say about that. I mean, I'm really honored. For me, I think what's exciting about that is because I really feel like the spirit of the studio is about giving back, and really enriching people's lives beyond acting. I think we're all about producing careers for actors, but it's really about creating community, creating a support network, and helping people in the business, and, like, there's a lot of love here. So, that's important.

                It's a blessing, you know what I mean? I think we're so popular because, again, I think people's lives change because of the work and they feel really supported. I think it's important that actors feel seen, and heard, and supported. And that's what this school's about.

125

Me:	Tell me about your method, because it's quite unconventional by most standards.
Anthony:	When I was coming back from Vancouver, on the plane I just had this weird epiphany, of, like, I really do feel like in many ways like we've ushered in a new revolution of acting training. And I don't mean that to be pretentious. I just mean I feel like it is so original, and I don't think that we've really seen a new movement in acting training since the time of Meisner and Adler. You know what I mean? Stanislavsky-based stuff.

There's no "Method." No Meisner, no Adler, no Strasberg, no Hagen, no sense memory, no substitution, no emotional recall, no imaginary "as-ifs," no back story and research, and things like that.

What we're doing here is really understanding the science. What I think is really amazing is there's a lot of neuroscience about where creativity comes from and how our brains are wired to create. So when I teach, I am helping actors understand that we're all hard-wired to create, but we get in our own way because of left brain stuff. And so, it's really about the science of the moment. If we can begin to understand how presence and being available to the moment changes us, 99.9% of the things that you're wanting are gonna be accessible to you.

My whole philosophy is that I think that all teachers who are really good see that it comes down to the moment, but for some reason I think a lot of teachers are still invested in the way things have been said for so long because that's the way it's been done. But I'm not. I'm interested in expanding our thoughts forward, in our consciousness expanding.

It's 2013. The demands for actors have changed so greatly, that for me to be teaching something from the 1980s is not applicable. For me to be teaching something that is not alive and changing is a dead teaching. And my teachings are always changing. I have to keep ahead of the curve.

It's universal. It's accessible for all of us because it's universal, but it's unique to each individual, because of who you are and what's special about you, what's weird and funny and messed up and beautiful and sexy and different about you, is different than me. It's all about how does that stuff get activated in the moment?

I realized that a lot of the things that we have been taught to spend our time doing is just busy-work. And that we feel like we're *really creating, and learning and growing and the craft of acting...* when it's just, literally, moving pieces of paper around on a desk.

Me: Do you think, then, that traditional acting teaching is dead and useless? Is there still any reason to go to a two or three year conservatory or pursue a degree?

Anthony: Stanislavsky, on his deathbed, repudiated a lot of what he had been teaching. And he was, like, none of that stuff works. However, I think what's good about, maybe, college training or a conservatory, is that really good programs give you a little bit of everything. I think that vein of it being a laboratory where you get to pick and choose and explore and discover who you are along the way, and then figure out what works for you— that's great. No matter what your training is, ultimately, whatever conceptual work you do, it's gonna come down to the moment. So, to me, the best teaching is about getting the actor immersed in the now.

Me: Do you think anyone can learn to act?

Anthony:	Sure. Yeah. Ryan Gosling says that there is no such thing as character, and it's all him, and he turns up parts of himself for a role, and he turns down other parts for himself for a role. And he says because he's always bringing himself to the role, everybody can learn to act, because it's essentially always you. And that's the truth. So, yeah, I've had people who you would think, "Oh, that person's never going to learn to act." But when they start accessing who they are, and then they bring that to something they're working on, for sure! I mean, we can all do that.
Me:	Do you think it's important for people to constantly stay in class, or do you think that for people who are getting steady work it's okay to let that go?
Anthony:	You know, I think I have two answers. One is that it's tricky because, maybe depending on the level of work you're getting... I have some students who are leads on series, but they find that the series that they're on— the writing and the demands for them— is not challenging. Or after three years of being on a show, they get stuck in a certain pattern of certain bad habits of acting. So they're not being stretched, their muscle isn't being stretched, they're not being asked to go into riskier, darker, scarier, more freeing places. I have people who do that, and then they come back, or they're in class still, and they're like, "What we're doing here is so exciting and then I'm on this series and it's not allowing me to do any of that." You know, they just have to say the lines. So that's my first thought: once you've gotten into the routine of a project, if you're finding that you're not being challenged and learning new things, I think you've gotta start finding something that's gonna stretch you.

And I think then, if you're on a really great cable show, or doing really great independent movies, for sure that's gonna stretch you.
I think really good actors want to be challenged. I |

have an actor right now that's pretty well known, and he just started in the intro class. And it's just so alien to him, working this way. It's exciting to see him really struggling, because he's been able to get by on his tricks for so long but I'm calling him on all that, and he can't rely on his set repertoire. His heart is willing, his spirit is willing to be challenged and grow, and that's what we're in it for. And for myself as a teacher, my own growth as a teacher, as a mentor, helping to inspire people, only comes out of myself being challenged.

Me: What is your biggest challenge or obstacle?

Anthony: The challenging thing for me is getting people out of left brain, cognitive, neural noise that we create for ourselves. "I'm not talented enough. I'm not pretty enough. I need to lose weight. It's never going to happen for me. I don't have an agent. I don't have the right agent. My boyfriend dumped me. I'm too fat. I'm too gay. This can't happen that way." That stuff really gets in the way of allowing you to express yourself. Getting people out of their way is a challenge, but that's where the breakthrough is. We have to get in our way in order to get out of our way. (Laughs)

We listen so much to the stuff in our heads, it prevents us from actually being expressed with other human beings, because we think, "What are they gonna think," and, "They're gonna think I'm weird," or, "That's too much," or, "They're gonna think I'm coming on to them," or, "That's too personal. " Those things are what keep us locked in the prison of our own private hell.

Me: What do you think holds actors back from getting work? Is it all of this stuff we're talking about?

Anthony:	Yes, all this stuff that we're talking about. The mental noise in our brains, in our left brain, really makes us think that we're not capable, we're not talented. It's our internal dialogues that the left brain generates.

But also, we compare ourselves to mythology. And I'm all about breaking myths. The media's job, especially in Hollywood, is to spin the finished product of what something looks like. So you see the billboards of the next new movie, or you see the trailer, or you go to the movie and you see Meryl Streep at her finest, and all these people are wonderful, *but you're comparing your dress rehearsal to their opening night. And all you see is their opening night.*

So you don't see along the way that she fell down, and she didn't believe she could do it, and she was challenged. And on set, there were probably a lot of bad takes, and sometimes she didn't know what to do and the director helped her, and maybe she felt like she phoned it in… But you don't see that! So then you compare yourself to a myth, that those people who've "made it" have something that you don't have. And it drives me bananas because the perpetuation of that myth, to me, creates more of the haves versus the have-nots. And that makes me really sad, because it should be a level playing field. A lot of other people who have huge careers are not any more talented than anybody else They've had good fortune, and they've been able to deliver the goods, and it's luck that the right project finds them. But most people think in those terms. It's really important to remember that.

I think what's exciting is the way the business is changing. It's like wild west out there with social media and new platforms for creating content. It creates more opportunities for people who can generate work, and you don't have to be famous to generate work.

When you dismantle the mythology of fame because fame is always going to drive our business. And again, it's created in myth. Look. American culture is so new. It's not hard-wired like Greek's, or you could even say, like, English aristocrats, who have the king and the queen and they have royalty, right? And Native Americans— they have shamanism. Most other cultures have myth. We're so young, we don't have myth, and so I think Hollywood is our myth. So we look to famous people as archetypes, and we think, "Once I have that, my life is gonna be amazing and blessed and problem-free." And so we become culturally obsessed with that fame.

Me: Based on what you just said about myth and culture and fame, what's the best advice you can give actors, especially who are just starting out?

Anthony: I think what's really important is to deconstruct that myth, and realize that whoever the actors are that you're inspired by, I think they broke through because they did it their own way. They're very unique individuals. The thing that I'm teaching is that you have to trust that you're enough, because we don't have *you*. We have other people trying to be like Cate Blanchett, but there's only one Cate Blanchett.

So it comes back to training, it comes back to understanding that we want to see who you are— who you are and the way you do this role— that creates the character. Character isn't on the outside-in. It's inside of you shining out. If you can harness that, and realize what's messy and weird and funny and fucked up and beautiful about you, that is what's gonna make you stand out…. And it's not about trying to *do* something. That's the other thing. You don't stand out by *doing* something, you just stand out by allowing who you authentically or essentially are to just *be*. That's so hard, though. It's vulnerable.

131

When I was twenty, I didn't like myself. I didn't love myself, I didn't know who I was. And again, I constantly use those reference points of "I had to look like him and be like him and have that body and look that way in order to be loved and accepted and get work." That was all rubbish. Once I began to really stop running away from who I was in life, and in my work, I began to get work. Because there was a place for Tony, you know?

So my advice is don't listen to anybody telling you that you have to do it *that* way. You do it your way. But you've gotta also be patient. It does not happen overnight. Careers take a long time. But actors are impatient about that.

Me: What is the key to career longevity?

Anthony: It depends on how you define career. Are we going for a commercial, societal model of what a successful career looks like? Meaning you have huge movies, tentpole movies that come out every year, every summer you're in a blockbuster? Because if we're looking at that, a successful career would be like Tom Cruise who does stuff that works for him. He's mostly in formulaic movies, tentpole movies that are big-budget, and good for him. So that has created career longevity…

I guess one could also say that the interesting thing about the business is that it sometimes does not allow people to move beyond the way they're seen and stereotyped. Tom Cruise has gotten himself stereotyped based on kind of strong action figure leading men. So that's what he does. He reinvents himself in those movies the same way. But that's created a career, right?

Maybe career longevity for somebody else could be doing work that is fulfilling, and really exciting, and constantly stretching you, and is dangerous, and tests how far you can go. And you know, you're respected, and you make a living at it.

My whole philosophy is that we're not really— we think we're doing it for the money and the bling and the babes and the boats and the material stuff, and then once you get all that, you realize that's not the reason we're creating at all. It's really for the experience of creating. It's connection. Creation is connection with other people. It's collaboration. And so, to me, a successful life means you're going for it.

What's success mean anyway? If you're going for your dreams and you're doing everything that you can, there's joy in it. There's joy in trying to break through. There's joy in going out and auditioning.

That is so important but we lose sight of the process. That's why we're doing it. So, it depends on how you define these things.

Me: What should actors do to be more proactive about their careers?

Anthony: You've gotta be in class. I'm not just saying that because I have a studio. You've got to generate your own work. Start writing. Put something up online. Do a play. Do readings of stuff. Read plays. You've gotta keep creating.

Also, part of being at a really good studio is— what we offer here is not only are people in classes, but every week there's casting directors that come in, and agents, and managers. So you can get in front of people.

Listen, it's like dating. Not everyone is gonna get you, so you have to cast a wide net, but everyone who comes in, industry professionals who are good, they

133

can impart information, and wisdom, and insight about things that you can also be doing and that you need to correct.

I think it's important for actors to train. If nothing else, to understand who they are. I think it's really healing and cathartic. I think that's also part of the gift and responsibility we have as artists. Artists, to me, are the wayshowers. We are showing the rest of the planet how to be. If we're not gonna do it, who is? It's artists! Artists are leading the way.

It makes me sad when I meet actors, and I'm like, "How long have you been here?" and they're like, "Oh, six years," and I'm like, "Well, what have you been doing," and they've never taken a class.

Let's say you don't know what you're doing, and you don't take a class, or you don't understand how a set works, and then you get a job. Well then what the fuck is gonna happen when you're on set? You know what I mean? It's gonna be crisis, you're gonna, like, defecate in your pants! What are you gonna do when you're working opposite Tom Cruise, or whoever it is, if you don't know what you're doing?

Me: Do you have any parting thoughts?

Anthony: You know, it's called a play. It's a play. Play. Play. Play. If you're not gonna do it and stay connected for the joy of doing it, then something's wrong. Again, this whole philosophy that it has to be so *hard*, and you just have to always talk about acting, and breathe acting, and live acting twenty-four-seven... No, you don't! It's not that big of a deal. It's just not. I have great respect for what the moment brings up for people, and the bravery it takes to share yourself in a vulnerable way, but that doesn't mean we have to be precious about it or masturbatory about it, or, you know.... finding a cure for cancer, and dealing

134

with cancer patients... That's drama. The Boston Marathon— the bombing— that's drama, and that's really serious! Acting, and this career, does not need to be. I'm not saying you should not take it seriously and not be responsible. You need to show up, and be integrous, and do your work, and take the career seriously, but this is supposed to be FUN!

I think we can get lost in the drama of it, and it's all bullshit to me. You know what I mean? It's like, you have champagne problems. If you've moved from South Dakota, and you could afford to get here, and now you're here and you have a lovely apartment on Hollywood Boulevard (you may be sharing the room with three other roommates), but you have a car and you're waiting tables at a restaurant and you can afford classes and you're going out on auditions and you've booked a few commercials and maybe you're getting a chance to go in and read for *Mad Men*.... That is a blessed life. Don't make it a source of pain and drama and conflict. It's important to remember that.

* * *

Anthony's best-selling book, **At Left Brain Turn Right** *is available on Amazon.com. For more information about his classes,* visit **www.AnthonyMeindl.com.**

Brian Reise,
Brian Reise Acting Studio

Brian Reise has been teaching acting classes in Los Angeles for 30 years and his passion clearly lies in taking actors of all levels and teaching them the vital skills necessary for building and sustaining a career in Hollywood.

He is a native Californian who has spent forty years in the entertainment industry. This wide range of first-hand experience has helped craft his teaching style and made him an approachable, personable, honest, and extremely knowledgeable teacher.

Brian's acting training included some of the best teachers from both coasts. He studied with Uta Hagen, Sandy Dennis, Bill Hickey, Lee Strasberg and Michael Shurtleff.

He has an excellent reputation for providing students with a practical approach to auditioning and on-set acting techniques and protocol. The skills acquired in Brian's classes directly benefit a students future and builds their confidence.

Whether a student is new to the business or a working professional, Brian Reise Acting Studios makes a positive difference in each individual's lives.

Me: Why did you decide to be a teacher, because you were an actor at one point?

Brian: I was an actor studying with a guy in New York named Michael Shurtleff. He was a big famous acting teacher there and when I moved back to LA, Michael subsequently moved to LA as well and asked me to teach for him. That is exactly how it happened. I only taught for him for three months. Here's why: A student in the class I was teaching for Michael — who, by the way, is still currently in my class with his twentyone year old daughter, who wasn't even born at that time— full circle— he said to me, "Hey the class wants us to be our own class, come and you can teach in my living room." For maybe the first year or two of my teaching, I taught in this guy's living room in the Valley.

Me:	Do you classify yourself as an acting teacher, a scene study class, an audition coach or is it just all of it?
Brian:	I am an acting teacher who teaches audition skills to get the job and acting skills to do the job. I prefer teaching classes to audition coaching. My teaching staff coaches for auditions all the time.
Me:	What I think is really interesting about your class that sets you apart from a lot of other teachers is that you actually watch TV shows and you pick apart what they are doing. Then you have the actors do that with scenes. What is it that you get out of that technique that you don't get with other kinds of teaching methods?
Brian:	Practical application. Truth. What you see is what you do. The actors you see on TV or in movies are employed. Your goal as an actor is to be employed. So do what the working actors are doing!
	My biggest challenge with most institutionalized education is whether it has *any* relevance to the student's future. As you know, my focus is all about what actors need to do in order to book a job. My class curriculum is focused only on what an actor will experience in real life in order to create and sustain an acting career. From the casting office experience, in terms of getting a job and going one-on-one with the casting director to being called back for in a producer's session, to advancing to a network session or meeting with studio execs, to being cast and working on set.
Me:	You actually have a lot of working actors— consistently working actors— in your class. Why is that?
Brian:	I think it's a couple of reasons. My classes are fun and supportive. I think that is the biggest difference between my studio and many classes in this town— too many acting classes are over-serious. Taking

the "art" aspect a little bit too far. I think for a lot of people, at least my students who are working actors, they like to go to a class that's like a gym. Work out, keep oiled, keep fresh and tuned up. They feel ready, confident and prepared when opportunity knocks. Instead of calling me in a panic after they have blown one of their best opportunities. "I was so rusty and nervous, I haven't been in class in so long, I felt terrible, I didn't make any choices, blah-blah-blah."

You would never, ever hear about a professional athlete who didn't work out, who didn't play their game year round. Day in, day out. It's not like, "Oh, I played one baseball game today and I have another game in three months. I'm good. I'll be just as good in three months without working out or practicing". Actors, when they are not acting, they are not improving or staying in shape. They can't improve at home, by themselves. It's not like a guitar you can practice on your own. Actors need an audience. They need to be in front of people to really feel the same juice, energy and nerves that are guaranteed in the market place. You need to be competitive. Just like an athlete.

Me: With the advent of YouTube and other social media outlets, has that changed how you teach?

Brian: Not so much the Internet per se, but the advancement of technology in general. Headshots and submissions are accepted on line now, uploaded reels are crucial and self-submissions of self taped auditions are the norm. Webisodes now allow actors more of an opportunity to showcase their talents. Green Screen is a highly profitable genre yet actors have no education in any of these new tools of the trade. We stay current and we adjust our teaching curriculum and advice and guidance to our actors to meet the current needs of the business. We change as the industry changes to be a relevant and reliable source of up to date informative teaching.

Me: Would you say that actors shouldn't spend their money on a two-year conservatory program or a theatre major? Do you think it's not beneficial?

Brian: That's a personal decision for each individual actor based on what their desired outcome is. Some actors only want to do theatre, not film and television. Some actors only want to have a career in film and television. I would say that if you are going to do a two-year conservatory that you need to be thinking about moving to a city that supports a theater mindset. That type of work is not in Los Angeles, it's just not. I would also say that if you want to be an actor, age is very important. Your concern must be that the later in life you start in this career, the more roadblocks and challenges you are going to face,

Me: For film and television?

Brian: Definitely for film and television, without a doubt. Because you have too many people that have credentials, that have come up the ranks as kids and they already have done a series or two, five movies. And you have zero. In this current market, they can get stars for the same pay rate they were willing to hire a less experienced actor for. Why are they going to pay anyone, who doesn't have any real credits, when they can get a legitimate star for the same price? It's a tricky question that people ask me all the time. Somebody came to me yesterday and said, "I'm thinking about moving to New York. What do you say?" I said, "Do you sing and dance?" Because if you don't sign and dance, New York is as competitive as Los Angeles with one tenth of the jobs. Unless you sing and dance, I wouldn't be going to New York.

Me: What can you say to people who are just starting out, who are older? Because there are a lot of people who would say, "I'm at a point in my life where I want to just go for the dream I always had." What things should they be doing, other than class, in terms of getting the experience, getting seen, trying to get an agent, trying to get a manager, trying to get an audition?

Brian: It's a marketing and sales game. This is one of the major elements that I really punch up in my classes that I think gets overlooked in other class environments. The fact is, that you're in a business. Everybody wants to think of the acting industry as art. It isn't art. Turn on *Smallville*. Are you are looking at that and thinking this is art? Eleven years later and it's one of the most successful television shows in the history of television.

You are not looking at that show and thinking, "My god these people are so artistic." It's a business like any other business.

I tell people all the time, an agent gets ten percent of what you make, so ultimately they are going to work ten percent of the time. That other ninety percent has got to be supplied by the actor. Part of that, of course, is the job aspect. You go to a set and you are working at ninety percent.

The other part of it is relationship-building, as in any business. Presentation skills. How you present yourself in the market place. Are you on time? A major, major thing! People are late all the time! I really try to wake people up and inspire people— to get them to understand that this is a business like any business. That they are going to be the employee. A lot of people think they're going to be running the show, they're going to think, "I'm a star, I'm Tom Cruise and everything is about me."

Most everybody is just going to be part of the workforce. They need to wake up and know that they

141

need to run by the rules of the workforce, not by their own rules, not by, "I'm an artist and I do whatever I want to do."

It really is a by-the-numbers town— the marketing, the sales, the "How do I get further along? Who do I meet and who do I contact?"

I'm not saying at all that you have to kiss anybody's ass or kowtow or sleep with everyone in town. I am saying that it's relationship-building like any business. You need to move up the ladder, but how do you move up the ladder? You make relationships as you are moving up, and hopefully they help you. It's tricky though, it's hard. Especially in today's environment— very competitive. We've gone through a major recession. Four years and this town has been beaten up as bad as any other industry. It's not just actors, its producers, its directors, it's casting directors, it's everyone above the line and it's everyone below the line. A lot of people have been out of work for a long time. That means that they are going to service the people that have been in the business the longest first.

Me: I guess the way that translates down to the actors is, they are going to go with the actors that they've worked with more as opposed to new actors.

Brian: And the food chain has completely changed in the last five years. What you see now when you turn on your television— you see movie stars doing TV. Dustin Hoffman was doing a television series, Glenn Close, Kevin Spacey. These are Academy Award winners that are doing television. Because that whole concept of crossing that line, that's completely changed now.

What it's done is this: the movie stars come in and take the leads that the "normal people" would usually have. The "normal" leads have now been pushed down to the guest stars, the guest stars have been pushed down to the co-stars, the co-stars have been pushed down to feature players. They have knocked everybody down one big step.

Me: How does the newcomer deal with that? How do they get in? What can they do to be proactive and productive to be able to get that first step, or first foot in the door?

Brian: Much of it is work ethic-based. Many of these kids don't have a work ethic. They weren't brought up with it. They are brought up to go to high school, go to college, to do the most minimal job that they can do to get through life to make sure that they are happy, to show their parents that they got a degree, or whatever. They don't have a work ethic, they don't know the ropes, they don't know how to play the game. I hate to be as crass as that, but that's really what it is.

It's just learning a system and playing within that system. A lot of people are not taught any of that. There is no education about that. I say to people all the time that one of most critical things in this business is you've got to have a work ethic. You've got to be thinking to yourself, "I want to do a good job."

Why do people say, "God, the product out in the marketplace is so shitty. All the actors are so bad." Why do they say that? Is it because the material is so bad, the director is so bad, the producers are so bad? Or because people get lazy, they rest on their laurels. "I'm a star now. I don't have to go to the gym anymore, I don't have to be good, I'm a star, that's all that matters." What you see is the quality starts to get worse and worse. The acceptance of that poor quality is clearly part of it.

Me: Would you say that the acceptance of the poor quality in the marketplace is what people are seeing so they think that's the standard to rise to?

Brian:	Absolutely. I think that they think, "Look, if they can do it, I can do it." They don't have to put out any more effort than somebody else. What they don't understand is that a lot of these people they see, that they've never seen before— doesn't even matter who it is… You can say, "Michael Cera. I've never seen Michael Cera before he was in Juno, and Ellen Page was in *Juno*, and I never saw either of them before. They just got lucky and now they are movie stars."
	Then you IMDb them and you see that Ellen Page had a series in Canada when she was eight years old. She had been in the business for fifteen years before you saw her in *Juno*, but you don't know that, and so you think she just got lucky. A lot of people think that some actors just get lucky.
Me:	I think they hear of the stories like Edward Furlong or the late Brad Renfro where they get discovered in a shopping mall and they think, "Oh that's going to happen to me."
Brian:	Exactly! And that started a million years ago and it's continued down the line. It's a business like any other business. You are working your way up the ladder. To me, one of the most important things is that people have to put the word "patience" into their vocabulary. Because it's all about longevity, it's not about, "Okay I'm a movie star," and that's it. I think what a lot of people don't understand that when you're a movie star, you are going to work the least amount of anyone else. The movie star does maybe one movie a year, maybe that takes two or three months, maybe they do publicity junkets for a month after that when the movie opens up. They are working four months a year. That's it, and then they are going to charity events and parties, going to functions. All that kind of stuff.
	They think that some movie star spent a year of their

life working on some movie, when, in reality, they might have done two weeks on that movie. People really think that they must have been all-consumed and doing all kinds of research for the character. Then you find out they only worked two weeks on the film.

Me: Have you ever had anybody in class that you just knew that they were going to make it, and has made it. Or you just saw something in them that like, "Man, that's the person." Does it exist?

Brian: I get calls all the time from agents and managers saying, "Can you send me the next big star?" It's so funny, because the "It" factor is: one agent has actor A and can't do anything with him at all, they are worthless. They can't get him out, they can't sell him on any level. Then actor A now goes to another agent, and they go out and become a star. It's hard to say, because I see the "It" factor all the time and those people go nowhere. I see the zero factor all the time and some of those people become movie stars.

Me: Why do you think that is? What's the difference in what they do? Is it the acting?

Brian: Confidence. It's confidence without a doubt. Confidence sells. It's a major sell in this town. I read blurbs to the actors in class all the time that come from casting directors or producers. Successful people saying, "Hey this is how to get more successful." One of them I read this week was a very big casting director in town, and she was asked what wows her in the office when people are coming in to audtion? She said, "I'll tell you what wows me... Confidence."

I then say at that point, "Did anybody hear the word talent? Was that in there anywhere? Because I heard the word confidence." Confidence was number one. It wasn't talent. The second thing that she said that wows her is when people that know her show. Which means, how many actors go in to audition for a show and they have never seen it? They don't know what kind of a show it is. They don't know the style, tone, genre, pacing. They don't know anything! They are just guessing! Are there any chefs in this town that don't know the other famous chefs? No! They know all of them all and are familiar with their work. Sometimes actors tell me they don't watch television or they don't go to movies. "I hate television." This is your business! How can you not watch? Especially now that television shows are so accessible through Hulu and Netflix. You no longer need a television set to stay informed.

Me: What should actors never do out there?

Brian: They should never be late to an audition or set call. They should never have an attitude about the audition material. "This show is beneath me, this show sucks. I don't like this person," or any of that stuff. It doesn't matter what the show is. It can be daytime, it can be at nighttime, it can be Disney, it can be your favorite show, or your least favorite show.

They should never forget the importance of professionalism. That's such an important thing. Unfortunately, in getting back to what my deal is all about— my deal is about professionalism— most people are not about that. They are about, "Well, what's your technique?"

Honestly, if you are a jerk and no fun to be with on the set, or no fun to be with in the office, then I don't care what your technique is. You are not getting to the set. You can ask any producer or director in this town and they will say, "I will hire someone that I like that is less talented before I will hire someone I don't like that is more talented."

They are going to a job. They want to have a good day, they don't want to go and have a pain in the ass on set. Professionalism is number one.

146

Actors should never stop being courteous, being charming, being nice, being gracious, being all those things that we all should be, but somehow it gets lost in the shuffle.

Lastly— though I didn't say it, but you heard Ben Affleck say it during his acceptance speech at the Academy Awards— don't hold a grudge. It was a pretty important statement made from a very major player in an environment with all major players. That's a thought-out statement, that doesn't just come out of the blue. That means that along the way, as you are going up the ladder, be grateful, be gracious, and you can't go wrong.

Me: What do you love about actors?

Brian: I love that they want to entertain. I love that they want to have fun and live their life on their terms as opposed to going to an office and sitting for eight hours a day in a building where they never see the sun. I love that they are crazy. I love that they are fun. They are not straight and narrow. That has nothing to do with being conservative or liberal or any of that stuff.

You said earlier— it was a very interesting thing, about people when they're changing careers or coming into this later in life. I get a ton of people that are ex-lawyers, ex-doctors, ex-sales people that were very high up on the success ladder and they hated their jobs. They want to do something that's going to be fun.

Me: Do you find that people who come from those backgrounds get further because of their professionalism and because of their experience in business?

Brian: I don't know if they get further, but they certainly understand the process better, without a doubt. As do athletes, and any person that comes from a very disciplined background. I find that athletes have a better shot because, again, they have a business mentality and a solid work ethic— back to the work ethic.

Me: Then what is the biggest challenge in what you do as an acting teacher?

Brian: Trying to inspire people to not be lazy. Laziness is a big deal in the acting world. That's probably the biggest issue— trying to get people to change their ways a little bit, to care more about their product, which is them. To be more disciplined and to have more pride in their work ethic. That's always challenging.

Me: You have agents and casting directors scouting your classes. Do they ever send you actors?

Brian: All the time. As soon as an agent or a manager gets less than glowing feedback on an actor, they are sending their clients somewhere to get better. No one wants to work with someone that's going to give them a bad reputation. If I send you out as my actor and my feedback is, "He was terrible," it makes it that much more challenging for me to get another one of my actors into the office. Because now all of a sudden, the casting director, the producer or the director, they don't think my taste is very good. Because I'm sending them somebody that's C-quality instead of A-quality.

Me: Do you have any final thoughts that you would like to impart to the newcomers of any age?

Brian: Have fun and don't take this whole thing as seriously as people want to make it out to be. Enjoy yourself. That's why you got into the business in the first place.

           And know that it's a long haul, it's not an overnight

deal. It's very hit-and-miss, and a lot of people think if they burn into town, they're going to get a series in a month. I see that all the time, and that's just wacky. They really think it. They really think that they are going to be a star right away.

It's a great business, it's a fun business, it's like any business. The more you treat it like a business I think the more success you will have.

* * *

For more information on Brian's classes,
      visit **www.BrianReiseActing.com**

Patrick Day,
Young Actors Space

Patrick Day has been an instructor at Young Actors Space since 1993, joining its founders Diane Hill Hardin and Nora Eckstein. He has taught and worked with, literally, hundreds of today's brightest young stars including Emma Stone, Samantha Boscarino, Barry Watson, Zoey Deutch, Dillon Lane, A.J. Michalka, Aly Michalka, and many more. The school is considered LA's top acting school for children and young adults.

As a professional actor, at fifteen years old, Patrick was cast in the title role of PBS's *Adventures of Huckleberry Finn*. He co-starred with legendary talent such as Lillian Gish, Jim Dale, Frederic Forrest, Geraldine Page, Barnard Hughes, Butterfly McQueen and Richard Kiley. Not only is his list of acting credits extensive, he has also directed hundreds of plays throughout his career.

In addition to running Young Actors Space, the premiere acting school for children and young adults, Patrick travels throughout the United States to present coaching seminars based on his method.

Me: How did you come to take over Young Actors Space, and why?

Patrick: Young Actors Space was started in 1979 by a woman named Diane Hill Hardin, who is still a teacher today. She teaches a lot out of New York. She is going to be doing some upcoming seminars with us. She and Nora Eckstein started the space. They started the space in 1981 is when it officially opened, but Diane started in '79, so somewhere in there was when it began.

They were the first to really work with children professionally. You know, it was a different time, the '80s. There was always one kid on a series, there were four channels, and so even though our classes— and

151

they were limited to fifteen students then, and still are limited to fifteen— it would be one class and pretty much everybody in there was a working actor. They would go to set and come to class and would make sure the class was part of their journey.

I came on board in '92. I was referred to Young Actors Space through my agent because I went to college to study film and theater directing. I always wanted to teach, even when I was doing movies back in Nashville.

When I moved out to Los Angeles, I was working as an actor, but I always had this real passion for teaching. When I graduated college, I went to the Space, and I walked in, and literally the first day I walked in, I knew I was home. It was just this feeling… I was sitting in the office, then I went into this first class with Diane, and the stuff that they were teaching I was not getting at USC, which is where I went to college. I was like, "They're teaching twelve year olds the real nuts and bolts of what's going on. No wonder this place is great."

Nora and I were talking to Meredith over at Coast to Coast, and Meredith looks over at Nora and goes, "You know I love you, but you guys used to drive us crazy because you were the first managers—" because Nora and Diane were managers throughout the late '80s and '90s, "You two were the first people in this industry." And they literally would go with every kid, every client, to the audition, or coach them before the audition. They started coaching kids, which was unheard of at the time. She goes, "It tore everybody else up, you were the only people in the city doing it, and so we would get frustrated, because if we didn't have a client, if one of our clients wasn't with you, we always lost out to you guys because you had that hands-on thing."

So Diane and Nora had established that. Now, life is a lot different. You see schools everywhere, and they're no longer managing.

Also, as you know, there's so much content out there. There are not just three channels or four channels, so you have a lot more opportunity, but there's a lot more of a glut in the industry.

Me: How does that create more of a glut?

Patrick: It feels very whitewash to me. It feels like everybody has a webisode or a web series, and it feels like even with such great content like, for instance, this festival that I went to at Pheonix— every movie I saw there, I was blown away by the quality. Now, I would probably never have seen these films had I not happened to be at that festival. I just feel like there's so much content out there, and there's so much good content out there, it's more about how do you get it seen?

I feel like there's a lot of work for actors. But because there's so much more work for actors, and literally anybody can go into their backyard with an iPhone 5, and have the quality of stuff that's, you know, fifteen years ago, and you can shoot it. It's just, how do you get it seen?

Me: Plus with the abundance of content, and everybody does have a webisode, how do you find the good stuff?

Patrick: That's the other thing. All the flotsam and jetsam that's out there, how do you weed through it? Because you can also just put up a Facebook ad and maybe see something, and you go, "Oh, there's a buzz about it." Then you look at it, and you go, "Why is there a buzz about it? I don't understand it."

Me: You got to the Young Actors Space, and you knew you
            were home. How did it come about that you ended up
            taking over the school?

Patrick: I was sort of a closeted actor while I was teaching,
            because there was a point in my career where early in
            college, I was like, "Well, you know I'm not going to
            teach because it means if you teach you can't act, and
            if you can't act you can teach." Then there was a point
            in my career in college where I went, "You know the
            people that teach, the people that direct, realize that
            other people can act too." It changed my life, because
            now I have two passions. I still love acting. At my
            heart I love acting, I love writing, I love directing, I
            love producing. It's a passion in my life, but I'm lucky
            enough in my life where I have a day job that is as
            cool, which is watching these young artists bloom.
            And not necessarily the ones that are on TV, but the
            ones that come in that first day and can't look you in
            the eye, and a couple of weeks later start picking their
            head up and walking a little taller. That to me is so
            rewarding.

            Anyway, the year is 2008. You remember Comedy
            Tanks. Diane had, years before, sold the business
            to Nora because she wanted to go off to New York,
            and she had a couple of grandbabies. Nora took over
            and ran the business for a couple of years, and her
            husband, Mark, who is a brilliant man, got a job in San
            Diego. She came to me and said, "Patrick, we're done.
            The school is closing. You either don't have a job or
            you have to learn now how to be a businessman."
            That's how I came to take over. This was a passion of
            mine, and something I love, and it was time to not be
            a hippie anymore and figure it out, and, honestly, one
            of the best decisions I ever made.

Me: When you took over, did you continue the tradition of
            the way they taught or did you change things?

Patrick:	Well, both. I continue the tradition of the way they taught, and I did change certain things.
Me:	What did you change or what did you add?
Patrick:	What remained the same is we limit our classes to fifteen. I'm strict about it. We have a two to three hour class, but with my adults, we'll go five hours some nights. It's all based in truth. It's all a lot of sensory work, which is what Young Actors Space really was rooted in. There's a lot of Spolin, there's a lot of Uta Hagen, there's a lot of Meisner. What I brought, and I think what any teacher brings, is their experience. I've kept a lot of what was great about Diane and Nora, and as I've evolved, I feel like every time I work with a client, either in coaching or in classes, you're getting every set I've been on, every class I've taught, every seminar I've taught, every job I haven't gotten as well as every job I have gotten.

That's what I try to bring because I don't think there's one methodology that works for everybody. I think that's a huge mistake. To me, that's like feeding people line readings, there's no growth or journey for the actor within that. I think every artist works differently, and I think the three main elements are still the same: relax, listen, react. That's what the model was of Young Actors Space, basically.

I think what I brought in was a precursor to that, which is when you get a script, it's: analyze, memorize, personalize. You want to look at it, you want to get the material down so you're not in your head, and then you want to personalize it. That's all done before you go to the audition. Then when you get to that audition, you throw it all away, and you relax, listen and react.

Me:	What is the youngest student that you teach and what is the oldest?

Patrick:	That's also something that's changed and evolved. We used to never take anybody under six, and we used to rarely take a six year old unless they could read. However, what I'm finding now, because of the information age, is that kids are learning much quicker. A five year old today is much different than what they would have been fifteen, twenty years ago because of the amount of stimuli and information that's around. Now we will take a five year old depending on where they're at developmentally. It just feels like anything younger than that, just let them be. Let them be a kid. They're already great. All you're going to do is get in their way.
	With the adults, I teach adults up to sixty. Right now I have adults in my class pushing fifty, and what we're trying to find with them is how to find their inner kid and bring it back.
Me:	What are some of the challenges you face teaching kids?
Patrick:	This. (Hold up his iPhone).
Me:	Really? The iPhone?
Patrick:	Getting them off of it. Literally last night in my teen class, my new thing is I call you out when I see the phone out. You're here, we're present, we are having a conversation. To me it's a sacred space. These are your free hours to actually have to look somebody in the eye and have a conversation. Last night, I couldn't believe it. I was like, "You guys, you know this rule." They've been with me forever, and they're a great group, but they're a rowdy group, so my new thing is when I see one of them pick up a phone if somebody is doing a scene, I call them out. I say, "Okay, suddenly one of the Kardashians just walked into the room. Can we put it down?" Then they get offended. The other big challenge is the occasional parent. I had

a conversation with an agent who called me last night and I said, "Okay, I sent you these two kids. I love these two. They're awesome." He said,"Here's why I can't get them work. One of the parents gets in their way. I'll call casting, I'll pitch them…" I said, "Really, because I know the other parent, and the other parent is great." He said, "Yeah, well the one parent actually has gotten a child fired from a job because that parent gets in there too much and doesn't let the kid just be a kid."

I look at these two children, and they have a great look. They take direction well, and they're so fun to work with. As a matter of fact, I coached them for this thing— for a manager meeting— and the manager called me and said, "Did you coach them for this?" I said, "Yeah." She goes, "Well, I need to send you the tape." The tape I was sent…? The Parents had gone and re-coached the kids and sent a different tape, after I coached them and put them on tape. I literally sent a video file, and one of the parents decided, "No this is not what we want." I looked at the other tape the parents sent and I said to the manager, "Of course you're not going to accept them, because it was all over the top and big."

We're lucky because I've only had to ask one student to leave because of a parent in twenty-plus years of this. I'm really lucky. Usually if it's not gelling, they go away on their own. I don't have to sit down and have that meeting, which I hate to have, but I will if they're offending somebody else in class, if they're disruptive and they're just not into it and they're doing it more for their parents, then I have to sit down and have a meeting. I've only had to do that once in my entire career, so I feel really lucky about that.

Me: We talked about the parent, sometimes, being the difficulty when trying in to teach kids. But external factors aside, strictly talking about acting, and

	teaching, and learning, what would be the biggest challenge when teaching a child or an adult.
Patrick:	That depends on the age. A five, six, seven year old, most of the time, it's getting the eye contact and getting them to actually trust themselves. When you get to the teens, sometimes they trust themselves, but it's not who they are and they're playing something else. If we're talking about teens and adults, I think it's really getting out of their own way. They tend to want to be something either they've seen on TV or seen in a band, and that's not really who they are.
Me:	The kids that are five, six, seven, do they really get it? Because sometimes you see a kid on TV or on a movie and they're like a little adult. How prevalent is that? How much training does that require?
Patrick:	Not a lot.
Me:	Really?
Patrick:	I can think of a client right now. He came in at six and he works all the time, and he came back a couple of years ago, and he's been in my singing class. He, at six years old, was referred by somebody who'd been as a child— second generation I call them. I met this kid, and the mom was like, "This is so-and-so, my son," and he had this internal adult inside his little body, that I went, "This kid is going to work." He's never had an acting class, there's not a lot I had to do, just get him to memorize and let him be him. And he works all the time now. He just had this internal something— you hear the term old soul? You really see it occasionally in kids. But it's rare. It's rare and it's exciting when it happens.
Me:	Do you think it's easier to teach kids or teach adults?
Patrick:	Honestly, I find teaching kids easier.

Me:	Why is that?

| Patrick: | Because most adults that I work with get hurt emotionally more than kids. They take criticism worse than kids and they need more attention than kids. I'm talking about first-time adults.

Right now I have a great group of adults. I'm so thankful and feel so blessed for the group of adults I have right now because they're so easy that the work we can do really excels every week, but I have had years of adults that are much harder to teach than kids.

The kids— they know their parents are paying the money, they know they have to learn the lines when they come in, somebody is watching them to make sure they're doing their stuff. |

| Me: | For parents who want to get their kids into acting, what is the best thing they can do for their kids and what should they expect? |

| Patrick: | Best thing they can do is have their kids read out loud. Cereal boxes, even when they're on Facebook, read it out loud. If they're not in LA or if they're not in this market, find a local theater community, get involved in theater. Get around other people that are producing stuff. And expect a lot of rejection. |

| Me: | What's the best thing parents can do to help their children deal with that rejection? |

| Patrick: | It's a great question. If you don't put the pressure on a kid, like, "My mom says if I get this part, I get the new iPod," or whatever. Because that's not at all what this is about. It's about wanting to do it, and wanting to be passionate about it. If they're not having fun— it's got to come from a place of fun. |

Me:	What should parents never do for their child actors?
Patrick:	That's a long list. Never give them a line reading. Never step in front of them if they're going to meet with an agent or a casting director, let them do it on their own. Never tell them it's more important than anything else, literally, anything else. It's not more important than baseball, it's not more important than school, it's not more important than a family picnic...
	Make sure that they know that it's all about fun. If it's not about fun it ain't worth doing, and the moment they feel it's un-fun, or it's not fun to be in class, get out, find something else. Find charcoal painting or ice skating, or whatever else.
	But at the same time, I do think this is part of a kid's development. I think it's super-important to try this out. If you just try one acting class it will benefit because you'll either know "yes or no," and it sometimes it's good to know that from the very first acting class.

* * *

*For more information about both kids and adult classes
at Young Actors Space, visit* **www.YoungActorsSpace.com**

The Actors

Kathrine Narducci,
The Sopranos, A Bronx Tale

Before her amazing discovery years ago by Robert De Niro, and long before her series regular role on *The Sopranos* for eight years, Kathrine Narducci was a struggling, single mom with two kids working a blue-collar job at a produce market in the Bronx.

Although her mother, who passed away at young age, was a poet and singer, nobody in her family or circle of friends was in the arts. Kathrine was a closeted actor, and her journey from that part of her life to now is not only amazing, it's inspirational.

Me: Your story of how you got discovered is pretty amazing. Would you mind sharing it?

Kathrine: I was a single parent. I got *The Actor Prepares* and I got all these acting books. I was teaching myself. I would always entertain people. I was always the class clown, so it came easy. I was working at the Hunts Point Terminal Market as a biller in the billing department. I would always make everybody laugh and they'd always be like, "Oh, my God. You need to be actress."

One day, a co-worker came in. She goes, "There's an open call in the Daily News. De Niro is doing an open call for his movie, but he's looking for the role of his nine-year-old son."

My son was nine at that time. She said, "You should see if there's anything in it for you." I said, "No, I'll bring my son and then I'll use him to get in the door, step on my kid's neck, [laughing] and then see if there's anything in it for me." My son came home from school. I had the article about the open call at a local theater where I lived.

I said to my son, "Do you want to meet Robert De Niro," not knowing it wasn't Robert De Niro who was looking for a nine-year-old. I'm thinking, literally, it was Robert De Niro. I knew nothing about the acting world. My son was like, "Yeah."

I took him to this open call. Poor kid. We sat there at this cattle call of thousands of kids. We were there for four hours. He was the last little boy to go in. When he went in, there was a sign up on the wall— handwritten sign— for Calo's role. Someone came out and took it down and put up a sign for the "Mom" role with the times on it.

Then, as I was waiting for my son who was the last little boy to go in, the "Moms" started showing up. I was like, "Wow. I look like them. I walk like them, talk like them..."

When someone came out with my son, I said, "Just out of curiosity, what is that? Why are they here?" She was like, "They're here for the mom role. Are you an actor?" I was like, "Yeah, but not really." She was like, "Well, we're looking for actors for that role. It's an open call, but for actors. But you do fit the description. If we don't find the mom today, tomorrow's going to be an open call for non-union. If you want to call in the morning to see if we found someone..." I called the next morning and asked, "Did you find someone? I was there yesterday with my son. You said that if you didn't, then I can come in." They said, "Oh, yeah. Yeah. Come. We remember you." I called work, took another day off and went to the audition.

They gave me sides and they said, "Okay, just remember your lines and when you come in, we're going to audition you," not knowing the "Mom" was De Niro's wife.

When I went in, my cousin was sitting outside waiting for me.

The woman called me in, and she said to me, "Okay, when you are done with these sides, just put them on the side. The cameras are going to keep rolling and I want you to tell me who you are. Just put them down and then just say, 'My name Kathrine Narducci,' and tell me who you are."

I said, "Me? I don't have a stop sign." For me, that was like, "You want to know who I am? I'm going to tell you who I am." I did the audition and I put the sides down. I looked in the camera and I said, "My name is Kathrine Narducci. I work at the Hunts Point Terminal Market, but I was born to be here. I was born to be an actress. I was born to do this. Every job I've ever had in my life, I know that I wasn't supposed to be there. I'm supposed to be here. My mother died when she was 49 of a heart attack. My father was murdered at 34. My daughter's father died before he knew I was even pregnant. I found out two weeks later I was pregnant after he died. My father's father was a junkie. That's who I am."

My cousin, who was peeking through the door, came walking in, rolled up the sides that were out there and hit me over the head and looked at me and said, "Tell her she's crazy. She shouldn't be here. That was crazy."

The casting director, who is a huge casting director, Ellen Chenoweth, looked at my cousin and said, "She's not crazy. She's supposed to be here and she was very good." I said, "Could I do that last part over again? I don't know if I should have said all that."

Ellen said, "No, thank you." I totally thought I'm not getting this."

I was getting dressed for work the next day and I was blowing my hair and talking to my cousin, who was there. My phone rang. I picked it up. I put the blow dryer down and I said, "Hello."

"Hi, Kathrine. This is Ellen Chenoweth. Bob saw your tape. He wants to know if you can come down tomorrow and meet him."

I was like, "Who's Bob? Who's this?"

"This is Ellen and you came and you auditioned yesterday. Well, Bob saw your tape. Robert De Niro." I was like, "What?" and I hung up on her. I looked at my cousin and I said, "You suck."

My cousin goes, "What are you talking about?" I was like, "You made someone call me?" She goes, "I didn't make anybody call you."

The phone rang again and I picked it the up. I said, "Hello."

"Hi, Kathrine. This is Ellen Chenoweth. I don't know. We got disconnected, but are you available to meet Robert De Niro tomorrow?"

I'm looking at my cousin and I was like, "Are you serious?" She was like, "Yeah. Bob saw your tape. He saw it and wants to meet you tomorrow." I was like, "Oh, my God. Yes! Yes!" I started screaming.

My cousin was like, "I can't believe this is even happening."

When I got there it was another cattle call. Therer were like 2,500 girls there. It was at the penthouse of Tribeca. My aunt came with me and it was going to be the same sides that I had, the same audition.

I was sitting and waiting with my aunt, and just like my son, I was the last one to go in. I was down there

166

for about— I'm not joking— six hours. Everybody had headshots and was very professional-looking.

I kept looking up. It was the penthouse— like an atrium— and up one level, you see doors. I kept looking at the doors open and I knew that the next person would go in. At one point, when I looked up and it was De Niro. He looked down and I looked up. He waved and I just went, "Oh, my God. Robert De Niro is looking off the balcony."

My aunt looked up and said, "Oh, hello." He was like, "Hey." He went back in and they go, "Kathrine Narducci?"

Now, this is crazy. When I talk about manifesting and law of attraction and all that kind of crap, when my mother was alive, my mother was obsessed with the movies and everything. Her favorite actor in the world was Robert De Niro. My mother used to watch *Mean Streets* and *The Godfather*. She would say "You've got to be an actress. You should be an actress. Be an actress." She would tell me, and have these fake auditions with me, and we would play. "You've got to be an actress because I want to meet Robert De Niro."

When I was walking up those steps, I started to get really nervous. It's the penthouse so the whole top is the skylight. That day, the sun was coming in. As I was walking up, I was like, "Oh, my God. I'm going to faint."

All of a sudden, that door opens up and I know that when that door opens, I'm going to see him.

I walked in the room and Chazz Palminteri standing there. I looked over at Chazz and he's like, "Hey, how are you? Say hi to Bob."

I'm like, "Oh, my God. I'm so nervous. I think I'm going to faint."

Bob goes, "You're supposed to be nervous. You're meeting me. Sit down." Bob goes and he gets me a glass of water. Then he says, "Okay. Look, I want you to know you're here for one reason. You told the truth yesterday. I'm talking about after. You know what you said? That's why you're here." He goes, "You were honest with me, and I just want you to just be honest right now. You read this the same way you read it yesterday." I said okay. I read the lines and he looks at me. He goes, "You really tellin' me the truth? Are you a good actress?" I said, "No."

He goes, "You're not lying to me?" I say no. He goes, "Okay. I want you to stay right where you are and I want you to do it again." I said okay. He goes, "But you're not going to read the lines. We're going to improvise. You know what that means?" I was like, "Not really."

He goes, "We're just going to get rid of the lines and I'm going to throw things out and you're going to organically say your lines back to me, whatever you feel." I said, "Okay." He sits back and tells me to come and sit on his lap.

I get up and I sit on his lap. He says, "You're just as beautiful as the day I married you." I got all shy and didn't say anything. Bob then says, "Hey, hey, look at me. You're beautiful."

I didn't say anything, and he tells me, "Go sit over there," and I sit down. He goes, "Why didn't you say anything to me? I told you we're going to improvise."

I said, "You told me to be truthful. Well, when somebody compliments me like that, I get shy. I don't really say anything, so I didn't say anything to you."

He goes, "I'm going to give you one last chance to tell me the truth, and it doesn't matter. Are you an actress?" I go, "No. You're making me feel like I'm lying and you think I'm lying."

He goes, "Alright alright alright."

He looks at me and all of sudden goes, "Stop screaming! Do you know how many fucking times I've had to drive that fucking bus back and forth to buy steak for this fucking house? That fucking kid, you can't take care of one fucking kid?"

I got up out of my chair and I went, "Fuck you!" I started screaming— I don't know what I was screaming. Then he got up and he starts chasing me around this coffee table that was in the room. I was like, "No! No!"

He was like, "Whoa!" and he goes, "Okay. Okay. Sit down. Sit down." I was like "Okay."

He looks over to me and then and Ellen. He goes, "There's a slight chance we may call you back tomorrow. Could you come back tomorrow?"

I go, "Yeah."

Remember the Instamatic cameras? He goes, "You want to take a picture with me?" I go, "No." He goes, "Alright. Okay."

I got up and I left. I didn't even know what just happened. My mother was in there with me. I go back home. I walk into my house and my answering machine was blinking.

It said, "Hi, this is Tribeca. It's Ellen Chenoweth. Bob would like you to come back tomorrow." I was like, "Oh, my God." I went back again and I did it again.

169

Then, he said to me, "Okay, here's the deal. We're going to screen test you. You're going to come back on Thursday. You're going to get a new outfit. We're going to dress you. You're going to screen test and you're going to do the same thing you did with me."

I go back and between hair and makeup and everything, I see two other girls getting their hair and makeup. I was like, "Oh." The girl who did my makeup— I said, "Who is that?" She goes, "Oh, they're testing, too."

I went over to De Niro. He's there with Barry Levinson. I walk over to him and I go, "I just need to talk to you for one second." He said, "What?"

I said, "I know that these two other girls and I know now what this means. I get it. If I don't do good today, I just want to thank you for everything. I want to thank you for this chance. You answered my question and made me know that this is where I'm supposed to be. I'm going to continue to do this. That's what this means to me. It gave me the answer that I should continue to do this. I just want to thank you for that. In case we test and then I just leave, I just want to tell you that."

He looks at my hand and he goes, "Don't ever trust anybody who says, 'Trust me.' But trust me. You're going to see me again. This is procedure. The gods in Hollywood need me to do this. They need to have that. You're my girl. You stay with me. You do what you did. That's it. That's what I need you to do today. Tell the truth. That's it."

We sat on the couch. We did the fire escape scene where I sit on his lap and we were done I looked at him. I said, "Thank you." They took me and those two girls to a room and he said, "You're going to get a call over the weekend, whoever gets this. I want to thank everybody. Thank you." I leave.

I go to my family's beach house in Long Island. We're there all together making dinner and the phone rings. I gave them that number. I said, "This is where I'm going to be." I'm holding a bowl of pasta and I'm bringing it to the table. I cross by the phone and the phone rings. I don't even think of anything. I'm like, "Hello," and it was Chazz Palminteri.

I go, "Hello." He goes, "Hi. Can I speak to Kathrine Narducci?" I go, "This is her." He said, "How are you, Rosina?" I went, *"What?"* He goes, "Yeah, Rosina. That's who you are." I screamed. My family goes, "What happened?" My aunt was like, "What?" I was like, "I got the role!" We were going crazy. We were going absolutely nuts. That's how I got it. That's how I got *A Bronx Tale.*

Me: Wow. Your life changed instantly.

Kathrine: Yeah. It changed because, first of all, it confirmed what I always knew about myself. It just confirmed it, but nobody I knew would help me confirm it, so you still don't know if you're a crazy lady or you're a dreamer. That was big.

When I did that film, on the set, agents were coming, like William Morris, De Niro's agents, and then a guy named Johnny who was a William Morris agent approached me and said, "Do you have representation?" From that day on, I had a gift handed to me, basically.

Then De Niro paid for me to go to acting lessons out of his own pocket for a year. He said, "I want you to keep doing this." I went to his coach that came to the set, Susan Batson, and then Sheila Grey in New York.

I quit my job. I had to become a waitress so that I

171

could wait tables at night and do auditions in the day. I booked a lot of TV shows and movies, like some movies and stuff like that. It just changed my destiny and my path.

It was like it was always waiting for me through all the trials and tribulations of my life, growing up dysfunctional, and all that. Because when it's your destiny, and something is supposed to happen— De Niro said to me when we were filming the movie, he said, "This is just so you know. I want to tell you this because you need to know this. If it wasn't for Martin Scorsese, I would be nowhere. I can't do TV. It's too fast for me. I think you're going to wind up doing a lot of television. But you're here because you're just supposed to be here. You said it yourself. You are supposed to be here. People are going to tell you, 'Oh, you are just being you. You aren't acting. That's you.' Well, let me tell you something. When you're at a wedding and somebody puts a camera on you and you wish the bride and groom well, everybody gets like, 'Oh, a wedding.' They start moving differently the minute a camera is on them. They do not act like themselves. It's harder to be yourself in front of a camera. That's really acting."

He said, "Remember that. You're not yourself, and it's hard if you're going to play yourself to be natural at playing yourself. You have the ability. You are an actor. You may have been in the Bronx in Hunts Point Terminal Market,"— these are his words— "in the asshole of New York, doing whatever you were doing. That paper had to come to that woman, that paper had to come to her for her to tell you because you were ready and it was your time. It was your ready time. That's it. Nobody can take a role away from you when it's supposed to be yours. Nobody."

I owned that. Everything he told me, I completely— Nothing stuck with me more than the talks I had with

172

him over that six-month period time, which was a lot of time to talk. That's it. I mean that's how it changed my life and my point of view on this business.

Me: What is your point of view on this business?

Kathrine: That it is hard work and perseverance and you have to have thick skin. You have to hear "no" a lot. When you walk into a room and somebody looks in your eyes and they get you and you get them, you get each other, nothing's going to stop you from getting that role.

I tell my students when I teach, "If there's anything else that you think you can do, then go do it. Then you're not supposed to be here." I can't do anything else. I don't want to do anything else. I would die.

Me: After you did *A Bronx Tale*, which was a major role in a major film with major stars, and you were starting to audition, and you did get a lot of nos how did you maintain your outlook, positiveness, having already done this major role?

Kathrine: I'll tell you. De Niro said to me when we were working, he said, "You're going to get a lot of nos. You're going to knock on the doors, you're going to get a lot of nos the same way I got a lot of nos until I met Marty. When I met Marty, when he opened the door, he got me the way I get you. You're going to have a lot of nos. Don't give up. It's not going to be easy. You think because you're playing my wife, that you're going to leave here and be a star, that's not going to happen. It's just not. You've got to keep at it. It's a hard business and you've got to stay persistent."

Me: What kinds of things did you do to stay productive and proactive during those times of auditioning before you got your next role?

Kathrine:	I actually went back to waiting tables and then stayed in class and nothing else. I just stayed doing a lot of readings, a lot auditioning in between. That was productive for me. As long as I was auditioning, that was productive.
Me:	Did you only rely on your agent to get you auditions or were you submitting yourself?
Kathrine:	No, because my agent said, "You don't do that anymore. You've got us, and that's how it works."
Me:	What do you think has been easier for you, film or television?
Kathrine:	I got more television, but let's not forget the whole thing about being pigeonholed. That was a double-edged sword, playing De Niro's wife because I was twenty-seven going on twenty-eight. I'm already playing mom. My friends are twenty-seven, even thirty, and they're not playing a mom yet. I was put right into that and playing a really ethnic, over-stereotyped kind of person. My youth basically went out the window. When people would meet me in person, all the time, they go, "Oh, my God. You're so much younger and different in person."

It was a lot of convincing and showing people I'm not really that Italian mom, and that I was acting. Then I got a role in *The Miracle on 34th Street*. I was a mom again and they would make me look dowdy and frumpy. Any time I was on screen, I looked 10 years older.

I thought I was a pretty girl. I had an unbelievable body, but I never got to play that. I never went in for the sexy girl because they didn't believe me or see me as that. It was just like, "Oh, she's a mom," and that's what I played. It was very hard. I guess now I realize, no, you don't have to do that. I still was very naïve in this business for a long time. I was working and making money, so I didn't naysay it back then because I was making money with it. My career was based on that.

Only now I'm fighting for myself, realizing I have to prove myself when I want to get on a show that wouldn't see me as another type of person. When they meet me, they go, "Oh, my God. I'm so glad your agent fought to get you in, because you're not what I thought." I have to fight because of that box that I'm put in.

Me: Let's talk about *The Sopranos* for a minute. You were on for eight years. What was it like working on a show for so long?

Kathrine: It made for a very comfortable lifestyle. I killed the role for Carmela. I killed that audition. Then I got a call two weeks later that they handed me the role of Charmaine. I didn't audition for Charmaine.

Me: What are you trying to do now to change people's minds about you so you're not stereotyped anymore as the "stereotypical Italian?"

Kathrine: I say to my agent or manager, "Let me put myself on tape for that role and I'll do it." They're shocked. Then, I get in the room and they convince them, it's like, wow, good thing.

It's so funny because any time I do go in for something that's not Italian, like even the *Beverly Hills Cop* series for a Beverly Hills detective, they couldn't believe it. As I'm reading, I saw the casting director was shocked about how great I did the audition. I'm more comfortable as an actor. I'm more playing non-Italians.

Me:	What do you think the differences are between New York and LA, and the process of the business?
Kathrine:	I think in New York, you're respected as an artist, period. You're respected when you walk in the room and they give you a fair shot. They don't even look at you like that, like "What was the last thing you did?" or anything like that. It's about the respect for the craft of acting. They respect actors and the art of acting. Whereas in LA, it's like a machine. It's like, "Who are you? What did you do? What do you look like? Blah, blah, blah."
Me:	Do you think it's harder in LA than it is in New York?
Kathrine:	Yes, because in New York there's more of a chance for even a beginner actor, a person who's just starting, who's not on the map, who's not a name in the industry. Yes, I think that they definitely respond to you better there.
Me:	You're going on twenty years now. What has it been like for you maintaining longevity in this industry?
Kathrine:	I would say it's having relationships. And also, being prepared when you audition so that the casting director remembers you and sincerely says, "She was great but she wasn't right for that. I'll remember her and bring her in for something else." That has happened to me.
	I think the longevity is mostly based on the perseverance. It's the biggest thing, perseverance. Not giving up. Don't feel jilted. Don't feel bitter. It comes through. Remember, there are no victims, only volunteers. You chose this. If you don't like it, be something that is going to have a paycheck there for you. You have to love this business. You have to.
Me:	What do you love about it?

Kathrine:	I love the process. I love the audition. I love when I walk into a room and somebody doesn't think I can do something and I blow the roof off it. I love it when I do a good job and I know it.
	I love the process of acting and I love the character study, and I love creating a character, and I love the whole journey.
Me:	If you could give any advice to somebody who's just starting out, what would that be?
Kathrine:	If you don't have self-love, you can't love anybody else. If you believe you're an actor eleven thousand percent through and through— if you believe that you weren't born to do it, you don't believe a hundred percent in yourself, then nobody else is going to believe you're an actor. I don't think you'll go far if you don't truly believe it.
	If you don't believe and know that you are an actor through and through, and there's nothing else you can do, nothing else *will* do. Nothing else.
	That's my advice. If you believe that you are an actor and there's nothing else that you can do, then you're in the right place. If you don't believe it, or if you have a doubt, then don't do it. Don't waste a lot of years, because in twenty years, you still might not make it. In thirty years, you still might not make it. You may be starting out at twenty, starry-eyed and wanting to be an actress and in your fifties, still not have an agent, but still love it and say, "I wouldn't have chosen another life," and not regret it. If you could still know that, then you're in the right place and keep doing it.
	You have to be your superhero of your own life.

Shaun Brown,
True Blood, The Newsroom, The First Family

Shaun Brown was born on an Air Force Base in Riverside, California. Growing up he wanted to be a heart surgeon but when he was cast in his first high school musical, *West Side Story*, he instantly fell in love with acting and continued exploring this new love.

He's a driven up-and-comer dedicated to constantly being productive and proactive about his career. As a result of his focus and determination, he is consistently working in television, film, and commercials.

Shaun has appeared in over a dozen national commercials, music videos, and danced alongside Latin legend Olga Tanon, in the 2008 Latin Grammy Awards. He can also be seen on HBO's *The* Newsroom and *True Blood*, ABC Family's *Bunheads*, and Nickelodeon's *Big Time Rush, Switched at Birth, Bar Karma*, and *Welcome to Harlem*, to name only a few. He has also done extensive theater in New York, from where he recently relocated almost two years ago.

Me: Tell me about some of your experiences that you've had in the two years that you've been here.

Shaun: When I first got here, I was staying with my best friend from college on her couch. I emailed a hundred and sixteen different agents and managers saying, "Young guy from New York, please have something to say to me. I can make you money." From that hundred and sixteen, eighteen responded. Then from those eighteen, I actually met with fourteen or fifteen. From there I signed with one— the guy that was the most passionate about me.

I really needed someone who was not going to put me on the back burner and be, like, "I'll send you out when I can." Someone who's, like, "I really, really believe in you." That's really important to me, and he did.

Me: What agency are you with?

Shaun: Mavrick Artists Agency for film and TV, and Abrams for Commercials. I've done a lot of commercials, national commercials. One for the Super Bowl for Samsung, and I did one for Jack In the Box.

Me: Did you start going out right away when you signed?

Shaun: I did not. It took about four months for theatrical auditions. For commercials, it was about a month. But theatrically I wasn't going out much, and then I got with a manager at Principato Young— one of the top management companies here in LA.

Me: How did you get them? Did you get them through the agency?

Shaun: No I didn't. I went to a casting director workshop, and this girl there— one of the other actors that was really, really funny— She was, like, "Do you have a manager?" I said, "No." She said, "Well, I'm with Principato, would you like me to send them your stuff?" I was like, "Please, God, do that, yeah!" He looked at my stuff and emailed me. We met for lunch, and it was on like Donkey Kong! From there, he got me an audition for a pilot, and I tested for it. It's a CBS pilot called, *Friend Me.*

When that happened, my agency was kind of like, "Oh wow, I guess this kid is doing well, let's send him out more." From there, I booked a guest star on *Bunheads.*

Me: Jeanie Bacharach and Mara Casey are the casting, right?

Shaun: Yeah, I love them! They are so good to me. They

brought me in all the time, and for that role, they brought me straight to the director. He liked me, and it was great working with Sutton Foster. She was amazing. From there I did *Switched at Birth*, just a one-liner, where I played a food runner in a kitchen, which at the time I was working in a restaurant. I was like, "Oh, I can do this. This is easy. Just say, "Behind you," and trip and fall.

I did that, and then from there I started working a lot short films. The community at University of Miami is very tightknit in the film community, and before I went to New York, I wanted to build a reel to show casting directors and directors. One of those guys, Miguel Ferrer, who is just a visionary— he's this up and coming director— was like, "You know, you've got to come to LA because I want to use you in this film which I'm now currently working on called the *The Fall*."

Me: Is it a feature?

Shaun: Right now it's a short film that he's using to pitch to studios to make into a feature. The budget was around forty grand, but it looks like it's a million dollars. It's unreal. The effects are amazing.

Me: You've had a very successful commercial period as well.

Shaun: Yes, thank God.

Me: Do you have a day job?

Shaun: No, I don't. This is it. This is it. I got some more commercials under my belt, and I went in to read for *The Newsroom*, and the casting director said, "You know what, you're really great for this, but I think I know what they're going to go for in this role. They want to go for a bigger guy." So I read for a different role. It was funny because she said, "Go out for five minutes and read for the role." What we do in Anthony Meindl's class, we take as script, we go outside for five minutes, we read it over and try to envision the circumstances as much as possible, and then just go for it, and I did it. And I booked it, and I just passed out when I found out. I was shooting that with Aaron Sorkin, who is amazing!

Me: He is a big musical theater guy.

Shaun: He is, yeah, he is. He is one of the nicest guys. I thought he was going to be a big, self-centered arrogant guy, because he has an Oscar and these huge hits, and Emmys, and he was really an actor's director. Even though he is executive producer of the show, he gave us some direction while on set and was very hands on at all times. I was working on that and then I got the audition for *True Blood*. My audition for that— it was just me and all these producers. I never even read for them, so I was kind of like, "Why am I here in the first place?" I don't know how that happened. I read for it, and Allen Ball was like, "That was beautiful," which I was like, "Okay. My character is supposed to be funny. I don't know why it's beautiful, but I'll take it." I went home, two hours later, my agency called me, and said, "You got that, too."

I was literally working from 5 a.m. until 2 a.m.— on *Newsroom* until 7 p.m. and then shooting over to *True Blood* and shooting that until 2 a.m., going home, sleeping for two hours and then going back to *Newsroom*. As tiring as it was, I felt like I was on top of the world. I was the happiest I've ever been.

When that was finished, I was doing a lot of waiting. I was pinned for the new Michael Bay Ninja Turtles movie. I waited for eight months and then I found out that they changed the script, which changed the

182

character I was hopefully going to be. I was always being called back and pinned for roles in movies and recurring roles in television, so it's starting to be really frustrating.

I have these great credits, I wanted to do the next big thing and it wasn't working out until recently this pilot season I tested for a pilot for TBS's *Ground Floor* by Bill Lawrence, who created *Scrubs*. From there he was like, "You know, I think you're perfect for this other role." We went straight to testing for another pilot called *Undateable* on NBC for Bill Lawrence.

Me: So you're perfect for *Undateable*?

Shaun: (Laughs) Yeah, I was like, "Cool! What does that say about me that I don't know already?" (Laughs) I went out for both of those and didn't get either one of them, and I was so discouraged. Right now I'm testing for another pilot for Adult Swim on Cartoon Network by Aaron McGruder, the guy who created "The Boondocks," it's a black cartoon.

My whole mantra that gets me through living in LA and being an actor is just focus on being the best actor I can be, because no one can deny me my excellence. They can say I'm too short for this role, or too tall for this role, I'm too black, we don't want a black guy, I'm too whatever— but you cannot deny that I'm talented or that I'm skilled. That way things fall into place, they'll start to bring me in for other rolls but also on top of that, is being the best person I can be as far as someone I would want to be around, because when you're on set for twelve, fourteen hours, it goes a long way to be someone that you can not only respect their craft but respect them as a person and want to work with them.

I think that mindset and my drive is what's propelling me, as people are saying, to this great breakthrough upcoming success that I'm having right now, which is unreal. I'm pinching myself every day and I'm like, "Yeah, this is my life." When I first got here and I was a bar back at this bar that I hated and not being taken seriously. And now I get to do what I love. It's an honor, man. It's crazy.

Me: Let me ask you this, because you've obviously had some really great success but you've also talked about how you've had some real disappointments, coming really close. You have your mantra, which keeps you going but for a lot of people who are starting out, or who have been here for a little bit of time and haven't had that kind of success, what advice can you give them? Because it's one thing to have a mantra and another thing to actually believe it.

Shaun: Yeah.

Me: Where do you reach down into to make sure you keep going, because there is a lot of "nos," to that one "yes?" How do you deal with that?

Shaun: I sit down and I write down things I have accomplished since college. My big accomplishments, just going through that and just writing it down and looking at all of that on paper and seeing it quantified. It just reassures me like, "I do have something."

Whether I was a supporting role in a Shakespearean show in school, or I shot this Indie film and the director thought that I was really great and was telling me that I was going to be big later on— just little stuff like that.

When I felt my most down, I could look at what other people were telling me, and that would bring me back up. Though I've had some successes, there have been times where would ask myself, "Am I doing the wrong thing? Should I have gone to med school like my mom wanted me to do?" I look at that and it propels me for another year. There's also this really great clip

184

on YouTube. It's called *Words of Wisdom* by Will Smith, who is a huge, huge inspiration to me. It's a collection of different interviews of Will just saying your talent will only get you so far, but it's your skill that will take you to the next level.

Just the hours and hours and hours of working hard, it's how he got to where he is, and all the "nos," and thinking irrationally. It's irrational to bend metal and sail it over or across the water, but thankfully the Wright Brothers and others didn't think so. Or to walk into a room and turn on a switch and all the lights would come on. Thank God Edison didn't think that was impossible. Just thinking about that and not living in "norms "or previous experiences— nothing really is impossible. It's your mind telling you it's impossible. It's fear.

Me: The inner voice.

Shaun: Exactly, nothing to fear but fear itself. That response to that a situation is what keeps you down. Tony says that a lot in his classes about the stories we tell ourselves, and how to overcome those stories. Because all they are, are stories.

Me: So, writing down your accomplishments...?

Shaun: Yeah. Also, talking to someone you really, really trust. I get down sometimes and I talk to my good friend, "I don't know what I'm doing, dude, I feel like I suck!" He's like, "Oh, yeah, you suck. You're recurring on two hit HBO shows and you have seven commercials running. Yeah, you're doing pretty awful bro."

Me: Nice reality check.

Shaun: Yeah, sometimes we need that. Also, I can't see myself doing anything else. When I get down, I'm like, "Well, what else could I do? Could I go back to med school? Could I go be a lawyer?" No! I would hate that, I

185

would hate my life. There's literally nothing else I would to than this.

Me: Let me ask you this, there is a lot of down time being an actor. How do you stay productive and proactive for your career? Obviously you have a social life, you do fun things, too, but do you do anything on a daily basis or a weekly basis to stay proactive and productive to help get you further to that next level?

Shaun: Absolutely. Acting classes, hands down. Especially Tony [Meindl's] class. He's very much a working actor's acting teacher and a beginning actor's acting teacher. Everything he says applies to the most fundamental and the most advanced. So being in class every week, and getting that jolt every week of being on my feet and really going deeper and deeper into myself is amazing. Other than that, the gym 'cause you got to look if you gonna be on camera (laughs).

             Also I like to write. One of my other goals and dreams is to self-produce some indie films to further the acceptance of minorities and women in, not only positive roles, but really dynamic inspiring and roles. Love Daniel Day Lewis, love Leonardo DeCaprio, love Hoffman, but I think there are roles like that for Hispanics and blacks and people who aren't recognized like that yet. So my goal is to do that. I have a lot of features that I'm writing, and pilots for television

Me: What lights you up?

Shaun: A character that is the most human of a character. Something really, really gritty and really real. Being ugly in a sense, instead of being "Hollywood" and glamorized. I really love those films where someone is overcoming something from the ground up like the film *The Pursuit of Happiness*.

Those kinds of films, the most human condition, so that we can hold a mirror up to society and be like, "This is what's going on right now," and hopefully from that we can spark change or inspire someone to make a change.

Also, on the flip side, I'm dying to be in some kind of really cool hundred and fifty million dollar explosions and aliens flick. I want to do horror films and not be the killer, but be the hero, not the first black guy that gets killed. I'm down with that too.

Me: Do you still really love musicals?

Shaun: Oh my God! Love dancing scenes.

Me: Coming from a musical theater background, how much of that has prepared you for this part of the industry? It's very different, obviously.

Shaun: Oh, it is. The technique of doing something eight times a week, being able to regenerate the energy— I don't drink coffee and I am a very energetic person. I think it's because of being on that adrenaline rush of doing so many shows and always in constant, "Alright, I have to go on and kill it and then the next day I have to go on and I have to kill it." Also, with that, I am so used to doing live theater that when I am on camera, granted the acting is very different, I can do it in one or two takes because I'm used to doing it in one take every day.

Me: Obviously to us it's different but for the newcomer, for someone who's just starting out, they may not understand the difference between theater acting and film/television/commercial acting. Can you just enlighten us a little bit on the major differences?

Shaun: For theater, I'll say how I approached it. It was very much the outside in, the physical-ness. I guess the analogy would be doing surgery with a scalpel for theater and then doing surgery with a laser for a film. You can think something in your mind, and then the camera can be on you and it's clear as day. If someone dies in front of you and you don't do anything but you're living in that, it'll be compelling. Whereas in theater you have to show the "Oh God! Oh!" and the tears and everything. It's just bigger. In theater, you're playing to the back of the house, way back of the house. In film, you're playing to the best friend, or whoever, while the camera is just watching us have this intimate moment.

Me: Let's go through the process of getting the call for the audition and then doing a test or booking a role. Can you break it down for us, and maybe define some terms for people who may not know them, like what's "being pinned," and what's being on "avail" or what's being "on hold" as opposed to "avail?" Then the screen test, obviously, there's sometimes a chemistry read and sometimes a pre-read. Can you just sort of take us through that process?

Shaun: In the beginning of my career— it's kind of changed now— but the way it started out was, I would get the email or the call from my agent saying, "You have an audition tomorrow for so and so casting director. It's a pre-read." Meaning you're going to read for the casting director, they're not going to film it and if they really like you, they'll bring you to the producer and put it on camera. So you do the pre-read, make your choices, do your thing. Sometimes you'll be called back later that day, sometimes you won't. That day or the next day you'll find out about the call-back, meaning coming back to the casting director. This time, maybe the producer's going to be there, or the director of the episode, or the director for the movie. And that gets nerve-wracking because you sit in this room and you'll either see everyone that looks exactly like you, or you'll see everyone that looks *nothing* like you. (Laughter) I've been in waiting rooms where it's

188

me a white guy, an Asian guy and a chick. I'm like, "What is happening?"

You go in there and at that point, honestly, your talent is still a factor, but it's also so many things like the look, and do you fit with what's already being set up in this world they're creating. Which I think is the part where people tend to get down on themselves the most—when they don't get those bookings after the callback, they think "Crap, I suck!" Maybe you didn't. Maybe you really killed it. But they wanted the white guy.

There've been so many times where I have been close. It's between me and a thirty year-old overweight guy, and the other guy got it, or a six-foot tall black guy who's overweight, or built or has model looks… It's always come down to, for the most part, they want a different look. Which I actually take a lot of comfort in because, "Oh, I did all I could and it had to come down to something I cannot control."

So don't worry about what you can't control. Worry, worry, worry, worry, worry, worry *about your craft*. Really focus on your craft, because that's what will serve you. Like I said, I've not been cast for certain things because of my look, but the casting director remembered me, or the producer remembered, and they brought me straight to producers the next time, or they just booked me straight to something else. That's how it works.

Then you go to the producer session and— if it's a pilot— if they really, really like you, they'll do the screen test, which is hell on earth.

Me: Why is that?

Shaun: So what happens is you get the call for the screen test and then you now have to negotiate your per-episode rate, which, when you're beginning is like seventeen grand an episode to about twenty-five grand an episode. When you negotiate it, you sign your contract so if you book this pilot, you're going to make this much money, it's going to have this many episodes and per season you're going to get this much of a bump. So you're like, "My life's going to be set. I'm going to get this boat. I'm going to pay off my house, pay off my momma's house, I'm going to get that car, that Lamborghini..." You're thinking about all these great things you can do. Not only do you want to book it because it would be cool to be on a TV show, but now you're thinking about the money that comes with it.

I first met with Warner Brothers, the heads of Warner Brothers, because Warner Brothers television is part of the affiliate for NBC. Met with them, I'm reading, some other guy will be testing with me. I'll go in, do my test, I'll wait for the other guy to go in and do his test, and we both leave. So it's kind of like, "What did they tell you? Did they say you did a great job?" You get so in your head about it. From there you wait and find out if you're gong to move on to the network test, which is the big Kahunas— all of NBC and Warner Brothers. Then you go to them and, literally, you're in this screening room and there's a light on you, and you're sitting in a chair and there's fifty suits all across from you on their Blackberries looking at your headshot and resume, sometimes not even laughing, or not even in the world that you're in right now. They're just picking you apart because they have millions of dollars invested in this project.

So you do that and then you go home and you wait for the call. You find out that day, an hour, two hours, three hours... and it's the worst. I like to take a nap, or try to take a nap, or I play video games where I'm killing a lot of things (Laughs) to get rid of the stress. "Call of Duty" is a good one.

190

	Then you get the call saying you got it or you didn't get it. I've never tested for a pilot where I didn't think, "Oh, hell, yeah! This is mine! This is mine in a handbag!"
Me:	But as you said, it comes down to something other than your talent.
Shaun:	For me— the one guy, he won an NBC showcase that they put on every year— he won it years ago and they've been trying to fit him into something. Then for the other pilot, the guy was already on a TBS show and they knew him. I'm still very much a baby to this industry. It's kind of, "You really have to take a chance on me." When you have the sure thing, I would book them, too. Now that I have these credits under my belt, I'm really excited about next pilot season.

For commercials, you go in and it's literally a lottery. It's like the demographic they're trying to reach. For that, when you get put on "avail" it's, "We really like you, make sure these days are open. If you book something and you shoot that day, let us know."

It's not a promise, they have no obligation to hire you, it's just, "You're in the final running." From there you either book it or you don't. |
| Me: | Then if they put you on hold that means they have to pay you because that means they're holding you for that day, but that's very rare now, right? |
| Shaun: | Yeah, I haven't actually had that happen to me yet. For being "pinned" for something— for instance, I was pinned for Ninja Turtles— they pinned me and they told me it's going to be shooting in Vancouver, here are the rehearsal dates. That also is no obligation for them to hire me, it's basically, I was one of the casting director's top choices, I had to meet with the director to see if he's keen on me, also. Being put "on |

hold" I'm told is that they want you and they want to make sure you are ready for those days.

Me: That's for TV or film.

Shaun: Yes. For instance, I'm on hold right now for a guest star for a sitcom where they're like, "We're using you but we don't know when our shoot date is, so just so you know it's possibly this or that day. If you book anything, let us know so we can make other choices.

I've never been on a sitcom, which is why I always test for these sitcoms and they're like "But you have no sitcom credits." I'm like, "I know, but I'm funny, trust me," and they're like, "But you have all these dramatic credits." That's the frustrating thing.

Me: Do you think maybe doing a YouTube video or Funny or Die video or doing something like that...?

Shaun: It's so funny you said that, my manager— we're creating a video we hope to go viral.

Me: I don't want to talk about the monetary stuff, but what drives you to do this and only this?

Shaun: What makes me want to do it in the first place is the power to really inspire and change things. I'm not a politician, I'm not a doctor but what I give, I think, is almost as noble.

People say we're not curing cancer, but in a way, happiness and joy is a great tool to coping. We might not be curing it but we definitely are treating it.

Digging into the self-exploration of myself and what I'm capable of... What keeps me going as far as this industry is concerned is all the naysayers. When I was in college I was told, "Don't move to LA, you're not going to work, you have too much of an interesting look. You need a chin implant..." All this crap that is always thrown at us. Even my parents, before I became successful, were like, "This is a hobby, you have to go be a doctor." My mom's a doctor. The"I-want-to prove-you-wrong" drive really keeps me going.

Me: That's good because for a lot of people that has the opposite effect.

Shaun: It does, it really does. But I love being told I can't do something, because it makes me want to prove you wrong. That's how I've always been. When I was in sports it was like that. In school it was like that. If there was a girl— "You can't get that girl" I'd be like, "Watch me get that girl." It's not coming from a sense of arrogance, just a sense of ,"You can't tell me what I can't do and what I can't accomplish"

Me: What is the biggest challenge in what you do? Obviously it's getting that breakthrough, but on a day-to-day basis, what's the biggest challenge for you?

Shaun: Really giving it my all each and every time. When I first started, sometimes I'd be like, "I'm going to phone it in this time," but there's no room for that. Especially now with YouTube, anyone can get a chance. I've been studying acting since I was 16 and someone puts up a video and they're in these movies with these critically acclaimed actors and directors. Argh! It kills me!

Also, though, because of the economy, and this really crazy shift in Internet programming, and these great TV shows— at first TV wasn't the thing to do. Now you have all these great shows like *Breaking Bad, Mad Men* and *The Newsroom* which are also being saturated by stars, so it's kind of hard for the up-and-comer to get these awesome rolls. Hearing that all the time— that they want the name— is hard.

Me: What do you think the actors just beginning or

just out of school need to do to be productive and proactive to get where you're currently at?

Shaun: I researched my butt off, meaning I signed up for IMDb Pro service, and it tells you the actor information and what they've done, their agent, management, the director and what he's working on coming up, or a script that's being optioned. I would take, for instance, Will Smith, and I would look at the first things that he did as an actor and watched the climb. Or someone that's not well known but I see them in everything and I'm like, "How'd they start out?" And I go back and I look at everything they've done. I watch movies that I like and I see how the acting is.

Like I said, theater and film are very different, so I study. Every time I watch something I'm studying it. Whether it be a cop drama, a sitcom, a romantic comedy, a horror film— just watching it and imitating it. Sometimes I will pause something I'm watching and then say a line like they said it, and see how does that live in me? Where does that come from?

Getting in an acting class, asking around of your actor friends or publications, like Backstage West, and seeing who are the top acting teachers right now being celebrated. Anthony was number one two years in a row.

Also, finding like-minded people who want to achieve great things. I think a lot of people come out to LA and they get with the wrong crowd who aren't driven and just want to drink or party, and they're like, "I'm out of college, I'm out of the house. I'm my own man or my own woman," and they do their own thing.

I like to surround myself with people who want this and eat it and breathe it and drink it and live it. From there you just in the bubble of awesomeness, and you don't realize just being in that, you're starting to achieve things. When you're in an acting class and you're getting better and better and better in your craft, and then an agent comes in and watches you—granted the agent might not sign you, but you are in their mind.

Get into student films. People will say student films suck, but being on set is, already, in itself a technique and a muscle that needs to be worked. The "hurry up and wait"— you have to get used to that because it's a beast. You can sit in your trailer for an hour and a half to two hours. I sat in my trailer for *True Blood* for four hours once, in my costume, just waiting to go to set.

Work ethic. You really, really, really, really, really have to go for it. There's no, "Oh, I'm going to try and do it." You can't be lazy about it, which some people are.

I find it all very fun. I don't ever get too tired. There's so much fun in the drive and the work and the pounding the pavement. It's a cool journey. When I do achieve something like *Newsroom* or *True Blood* I love to look back and be like, "Man, remember that time a year and a half ago when you first moved here and you were sleeping on your friend's couch eating Ramen noodles and you lost— " I'm a skinny guy, and I lost thirteen, fourteen pounds.

So drive, research, surrounding yourself with good people, get into a great acting studio.

Me: What would you say to people who aren't here yet and are going to read this book and they're deciding whether they should come to LA or maybe stay local in a smaller market. What do you think about that?

Shaun: It's funny because my friends ask me this all the time, "When should I move to LA?" Honestly? Move now. If you really want to do this, you really want to do it! You have to jump in the pool because the machine will run without you.

I have a lot of friends who are staying in their hometown they're like, "I'm going to get there, I'm going to get there." You can be where you are, but the business is going to keep on going, and no one is going to know or care. So you have to just make the jump.

Me: You refer to it as the business, and we all talk about show business, but I find that most actors are really good at the artistic, creative part of it, but really crappy at the business part of it. So having all this amazing success that you've had over the last year and a half and before that, what kind of skills have you had to develop to deal with "the business" aspect of the business?

Shaun: Coming into a meeting with an agent or casting director or director, like I said earlier, being a good person… a lot of people when they meet an agent, they hand over their headshot and resume and say, "So last year I did this thing, I had this kind of training…" Where, I personally want to get to know you. I'm interviewing you like you're interviewing me. Do I want to work with you? Granted, I hope you want to cast me in the whatever kind of film it is, but it's really down to showing up and having that personality that people are attracted to.

I'm very big on, like I said, IMDb Pro— looking at movies I want to be a part of and hitting up my agent or manager and being like, "How do we get into this movie?" Also knowing my brand, I know I'm not the Denzel Washington type, but I know that I can be the funny, nerdy, best friend in a lot of things.

Me: You have to know who you are.

Shaun: Yeah.

Me: And be okay with it too.

Shaun:	Yes! That's the biggest thing— being okay with it. I know later on I'll reinvent myself and I'll pack on the muscles.

Shaun: Yes! That's the biggest thing— being okay with it. I know later on I'll reinvent myself and I'll pack on the muscles.

This movie I was doing, I put on a lot of weight. I put on a lot of muscle and it worked for this film, but I wanted to keep it on because I wanted to try to cross over to the action guy, but my manager was like, "That's going to take another two years, lose the weight." Of course, I was really offended but I was like, "No, he's absolutely right." For what I have to offer, there's not many guys like me that are out there right now doing it. So knowing that and being okay with it, and coming in with that and pushing that product is so valuable— and understanding the business. A lot of people are like, "Oh, I don't like the way it works with the auditioning and the callbacks and stuff." If you really want to do this, you have to do all of it. Show business is not "show art." You have to know how to market yourself. You have to be good with that kind of stuff.

I launched my fan page, my Twitter, my Instagram… All a star is, is how much public awareness they have. I'm nowhere near being a star, but building that fan base with my Instagram or my Twitter or my fan page, having my work there all the time so that people can see it— and you never know who's looking at your stuff. Justin Bieber was found by Usher. That's crazy to me.

So being hip to that kind of stuff and not being so resistant to it, because I think it's important. We're in a new age now, you have to get with it and you have to accept it.

Me: Any parting thoughts for the newcomers?

Shaun: Just really, really focus on being the best actor you can
            be and the best person you can be. No one can deny
            you your excellence. They can deny you things you
            can't control, but recognizing a good actor, that speaks
            volumes. And get to LA.

Hemky Madera,
Weeds, Rango, Caribe Road

Hemky Madera was born in New York but was raised in the Dominican Republic. His mother came to the states just for a vacation while pregnant, and due to some complications, he arrived as an American citizen upon his birth.

But Hemky's good fortune didn't stop there. After beginning his first acting class in the Dominican Republic, he was cast in a mini-series.

Me: How, exactly, did the mini-series come about?

Hemky: This producer-director named Ponce Rodriguez, in the Dominican Republic, gave me my first shot when I was twenty years old. At that point, I've never taken any classes or acted professionally. I did one or two little high school productions, but nothing major. It was more like a credit more than anything else. Ponce gave me this gig because I auditioned for his class. That's when I auditioned for the first time ever— for a class. It was my best friend, Ron, and myself who auditioned.

Three weeks into the class, I hear that I am going to be one of the leads in Ponce's next mini-series. So we go celebrate, "Yes, Oh my God, cool dude, you made it, man!" Time passes, I hear nothing, but I'm like, "Cool, whatever." Three more weeks pass, I don't hear anything. They're about to start shooting on a Monday— this was, like, on a Thursday— I was like, "You know what, I guess I'm not good for this." So I just went with a bunch of my friends to the beach.

Back then, all we had was pagers, no cell phones, or they were very expensive to have a cell phone. So I leave the pager at the house, because I'd heard about the show at this point. And we're down there, and we're drinking, we're jet-skiing, boys being boys. I come back to the house and I have eighteen pages from a phone that I don't know. So I'm like, "What the... ." So I call, like, "Yeah, you been paging me?"

"Where the fuck are you?" And I'm like, "Who the fuck is this?" "This is Alfonso." He goes, "Hemky, we start principal photography on Monday."

I'm like, "What are you talking about?" He said, "Wait a second, nobody told you? I hired you from the first audition when you went to class." Alfonso told me he thought that the producer thought he told me, and then it was, like, nobody told me anything. So I run to Santiago, he meets me halfway, picks me up and then on the way there, I start learning my lines, reading the script, and all that stuff.

Me: How long had it been from the first audition to that?

Hemky: Six weeks, and I have no idea. In that moment, I was playing back conversations in my head, and little innuendoes and little stuff that he would say in class, like, "Oh, yeah, no, so Hemky, pay attention to this because you're going to be doing this." Eventually, I'm like, "Oh, yeah," but literally, I had no idea I was going to do that. So I did two mini-series with him. After that, I say fuck it. I went to New York.

Me: How old were you at the time?

Hemky: Twenty-two. I went to New York. I had no idea what the hell I was doing, and somebody told me, go to the mayor's list, there's a bunch of indie production, stuff like that. Try to get in as a P.A. So I did that, and I volunteered as a P.A. in a film called *Bookie's Lament*, which— it was fun, it was fun, a lot of work, you know... indie... free. I was a kid, I was hungry as hell, so they offered me a little part there after two weeks of working. "Hemky, just play this little Puerto Rican guy." It was fun, you know.

Then after that, I started doing a lot of commercials, P.A. on commercials. One day I just got burned out on working many hours. I went to a temp agency which got me an interview with Citibank with the international credit card department. I b.s.'d and I put on my resume that I went to college, but I never graduated. I changed majors four times and then I don't have a single credit in my name because that wasn't my calling.

I go there, sell myself. I got to twenty minutes, and the guy said, "Hemky, I like you, you're a good kid, you seem like a good kid, you're hired." In this whole conversation, I say, "I'm an actor." I never hid anything, hid that part, I never hid anything. Five seconds after I walked out from that interview, Ponce Rodriguez calls me back— by that point, I already had a cell phone— and says, "Hemky, now I'm the head of this network in the Dominican Republic. We're about to do sitcoms. I need you here tomorrow." So I turn around and say, "I quit." The guy's face was like, "Wait.. what?" I was like, "You're not going to believe this…"

The next day, I'm in the Dominican Republic. And that was my real school, because in the Dominican Republic at the time, they didn't have the concept of having a weekly show, like *Friends*, that comes out once a week or any sitcom, per se, or a new show. What they have is a soap opera mentality. They need to have a fresh show every day, so we were on set for twenty hours a day, sixteen hours a day, multiple cameras. In two years, I did two hundred-eighty episodes. So you can imagine that I had no life from Monday to Friday.

Me: What incredible training.

Hemky: Oh, yeah, it is. We were working with three or
            four cameras, three cameras all the time and then

	sometimes a fourth camera. So that was my school.
Me:	How big are soap operas in the Dominican Republic?
Hemky:	Soap operas are huge, especially foreign soap operas, especially Mexican or Columbian soap operas.
Me:	So you said the show you were on was a very big show?
Hemky:	It was *Los Electrolocos.* That was more for kids. Just recently, I was in the Dominican Republic doing a film and somebody comes up to me, "Oh, my God, you're Ricky! Ricky from *Electrolocos!* Oh, my God, I used to watch you when I used to come from school when I was, like, in fifth grade," or something. I was like, oh, my God, I'm so freaking old. So I did that for two years.
Me:	You were also famous back there.
Hemky:	The fun thing about it is... like I say, it was school. It was training, and then at the same time, Ponce also gave me the opportunity to produce another sitcom, so while I was acting, I was also producing. So I learned from both sides of the coin.
Me:	When you were auditioning in New York, was that stuff you were getting out of the paper?
Hemky:	Yeah, the paper Backstage.
	My friend Frank he looks in Backstage and there's this article about Gene Frankel. Gene Frankel was one of the members of the Actor's Studio back when. He was one of the— not founding members— but he was one of the first members of the Actor's Studio. So we start taking classes with him and I remember, we were broke.
	Oh, my God, we were so broke, and I was handing,

at this point, I was handing headshots and resumes to every casting agent, every production office. Then 9/11 happened and nobody wanted to open envelopes at that time, because nobody knew what was going on.

So what I did was I used to buy clear, see-through envelopes so they could see it was a headshot. I used to print the resume on the back of the picture and send it, and send it, and send it. I must have sent like a hundred, and nothing, nothing, nothing, nothing. One time, I run out of money and they cut off my cell phone. A friend of mine says, "Hemky, do me a favor, man, do me a solid. I'm doing this student film, can you help me out? It's one scene, it's going to take ten minutes." Haha, ten minutes.

Me: On a student film (laughs).

Hemky: Yeah. Naïve of me. So I went. I remember, I checked my messages in my home phone at noon. The scene took three hours to make. I checked my messages again at three. At 12:05, mind me, I checked my messages at noon ... at 12:05, *The Sopranos* called. The casting director of *The Sopranos!* It was a little role. It was mine. By the time I called, like 2:50, they already offered it to somebody else because I didn't call in time. And it was a little under five, which later I found out, that under five became a series regular, or a recurring, for three seasons. That was a low blow. That was hard, but at the same time, on that same day, we met a girl who talked to us about doing an internship at the Actor's Studio, at the original Actor's Studio, so Frank and I, we went there, we interviewed, we got the gig, and then we kept auditioning.

Frank and I, we got our first paying acting gig in New York City. It was at the Puerto Rican Traveling Theater, making $300 a week. We get the callback and after the callback, the director says, "You guys are hired." I remember, Frank and I, we walked out of there screaming, "Yeah, we made it!" For $300 a week! Then after that, I did a bunch of off-Broadway shows. Things started picking up there. But it was hard, man, it was hard, especially in New York, it's not about the looks. New York is about the talent and the craft.

Me: Had you had some theater training at all?

Hemky: I did one play in the Dominican Republic right before I moved to New York for the second time.

Me: So your training was really on the set of the show, and then you were in class as well.

Hemky: Yeah, but my first play, I had no experience whatsoever doing plays, and it was a three-person play. For two and a half years, I was in New York, just doing plays and plays, and I did an episode of *Law & Order: Criminal Intent*. That's how I got my SAG card.

Me: How'd you get that role?

Hemky: I got a manager for a brief moment in New York. I was there for a year and a half. For whatever reason, I couldn't get a theatrical agent. It was hard, really, really hard, because I didn't have the credits. So this manager, he sent me to an audition for *Law & Order*. I wasn't union then and it was for an under five. At the time, I had no idea how the process worked of how they see union. I went in and right away, I felt comfortable. I was like, "I have nothing to lose." I was hungry as hell, like this is mine. I went there, did the audition like I was already filming it— I was already shooting the scene. The next day, they say, "Hemky, it's yours."

I remember, oh God, I remember when I was on set, I was so broke. I was doing plays, but it was Off-Broadway shows. There's no money in New York for those Off-Broadway shows. It was a lot of experience, but no money. Then, the P.A.s were going around, "We're going to go to Starbucks, you want anything?" and I thought I had to pay for my Starbucks. I'm like, "I'm cool, thank you, I'm good, thank you." Then the P.A. notices and goes, "Please don't take no offense, but you know you don't have to pay for this." I had no idea. I had no idea how it worked in this part of the world.

So after I did that show, I just said, you know what, fuck it, I'm going to LA I'm going to be a film actor, TV actor. So I pack my bags without knowing anybody, $1,200 in my pocket and on the phone— a three-way call— a friend of mine from Denver introduced me to a friend of hers in LA who rents me a floor of his studio. He rented it to me, the floor, for $300 for that month. I bought a motorcycle for $700 and I had $200 left. So I was doing my rounds here.

Me: How'd you support yourself while you were here?

Hemky: I had one residual check from the *Law & Order* thing. Then I had a tax refund. So, pretty much, I was lucky. I wasn't working. I was looking for a job, too. I needed to work and I couldn't get a freaking job for the life of me, so all this time I'm going to auditions, I'm going to this, I'm going to that. At this point, I need an agent, so I call some people in New York and say, "Can you recommend anybody, anybody that you know that can talk to me? I need an agent." One guy says, "There is this guy, his name is Bob Waters. He's from here, New York, and he moved to LA five years ago. Just go there, drop your stuff. You never know."

So I call the agent, Bob Waters. I ask for the address. I get the address. I go there with my package. It's a one-man operation, the secretary and an office in the back. So I see the secretary, this elderly woman, very sweet woman, and I really just run by her, dropped my stuff on Bob's desk and said, "I know this is not the way to do things. My name is Hemky Madera, I just moved from New York. If you like it, give me a call." The next day, he signed me.

Me: That's great. Was he able to get you out on auditions?

Hemky: Right then and there, I start going on auditions. Of course, my first day of auditions, I had three auditions, and it was same-day auditions, because it was like that. And I did so bad. I was so nervous, for the first time walking into a studio. I'm like, "My God, I'm auditioning for JAG." I was so nervous. That casting director never called me again for four years. But then after that, I kept going and then the first job that I booked *Lost City*, the Andy Garcia film. But how ironic is this? My first gig that I booked in LA? Where does it shoot? Where does it film? The Dominican Republic (laughs). So I go back.

Me: What kind of role did you have in that movie?

Hemky: I play a revolutionary, a rebel. It was good. It was a short part, small part, but it was good. My scene was with Andy, so that was pretty cool.

           Then after that, I came back to LA I waited tables, I did everything and anything, and it's not easy. But you have to just keep going. Then after a while, auditioning and auditioning and being rejected, I get this manager. Bob Waters didn't like that, so he dropped me. So I didn't have an agent.

           For a while, I just had the manager. She got me some auditions, but all this time, I was just waiting tables, made nothing and did nothing. Then I met with Brianna at Clear Talent Group, and I'll never forget this. She just opened the department, the film and television department, and said, "Hemky, I might not have that many connections right now, but I will work for you and I will fight for you." Right there and then,

	I said, "Let's do it." She got me auditions and I kept auditioning.
Me:	What was your very first commercial? Was that before or after the Andy Garcia film? I'm just trying to get a time frame on it.
Hemky:	After.
Me:	Did Bob represent you across the board then?
Hemky:	No. At that time, I was with AKA. After I do my two commercials, the manager at the time convinced me to go to KSR, to meet with them. So I met with KSR and I thought those girls there were amazing. So I did the switch there and I used to go out five, six, eight times a week, commercially. I still do.

I booked, and then I'm broke again, and this happened for a long time. I always had my shield, "Nothing's going to ruin me." I booked this promo commercial— it was supposed to be a huge campaign, so I shot everything, it was fine. I was counting on that money. I was working, waiting tables at Santa Clarita, so I quit that job, because I was going to make all this money.

Something happened with the director and the publicist and everything, so everything just got cut-off, recast, re-everything, and I'm like, "What the hell?" That hit me hard. That hit me so freaking hard.

| Me: | How did you deal with that? |
| Hemky: | I think I went into a depression because I couldn't believe it. And I wasn't making any money. I was broke. I have to give up my apartment. So I had a choice, either go to New York again or stay here, but if I leave, everything that I've done here is going to be out the window. All the connections, everything. |

Me:	That's when you got with Brianna and Clear Talent Group? Is that when you got *Weeds?*
Hemky:	No, no, I was with Brianna right before that because I was just auditioning there. Then I lost the apartment, and I kept on auditioning, and then after ten months of being on a couch— and I was catering, and I was making money— I go to this audition for *Weeds,* for this mechanic role. At this point, I'm getting my groove back, I'm like, "Fuck it. Fuck it, fuck them, fuck everybody. I am going to book this shit. Stop feeling sorry for yourself and fucking go for it. You're not a fucking ... you're not a loser." I remember saying, "You're not a fucking loser, just fucking go and do what you know best." So I go there and I do my audition, I do my thing, and there's like silence in the room. I leave. Brianna calls me twenty minutes later, "They want to see you again tomorrow, but this time for a bigger role."

I went there for another role, a bigger role. I do my thing again, and they're like, "Whoa. Okay. We're going to bring you back next week again for the role of the mayor, but we're not going to offer it to you. You're way too young for that role. You're not right for the role. We just want to see what can you bring to the table." I'm like, "Sure!" A week later, I shave, I do my audition and stuff like that and like, whoa, this is a role named Ignacio.

They tell me, "If Ignacio happens, if he stays on paper, the role is yours."

I got the role of Ignacio, which happened to be two blocks from the apartment that I just got. I just pretty much walked to work. So I go to work, and at the time, I'm all excited. On the second episode— this is a scene with Elizabeth Perkins— I ask her to get me some Chinese food. I show her my gun and she goes, "Cock and guns, guns and cock, roses will be fine," and she comes to me and gets the money out of my hand, and organically, out of me, I blew her a kiss. I just blew her a kiss. That kind of threw her off and every crew member, one by one, came up to me and said, and whispered, kind of like threw it away, "You just wrote yourself into the rest of the season.

Next episode, they called me. Following episode, they called me. Then I had this huge scene with Mary Louise Parker, which— she's a hell of an actress. She never delivers the lines the same way. Always money on the lines— so we had this dance. She talked to the writers to keep writing for me so that two episodes became a three-season, very memorable role on *Weeds*.

Me: That's quite a story. So, basically, what you're saying is, you did something so interesting and organic, just because of all your training and being on the set and what you've done in New York, that in that moment you created an entirely new future for yourself.

Hemky: In that moment. I could have just said the lines as they were, as the character was supposed to be, but then on all this meanness, I did a little switch and I just blew her a kiss. That little thing just changed the character and it became one of my most memorable works over three seasons.

Me: How have things changed for you— from feast one day, famine the next— from recurring on *Weeds* for three seasons?

Hemky: Don't get me wrong, now things are interesting because I'm up against people with more credit than me, bigger names. Now I'm in that bubble, but little by little, just keep hacking at it. The moral of the story is don't let anybody— nobody, not even yourself— stop you from your dreams. It's not easy because we, as artists, have our own demons. There is no more critical person than ourself, and we put ourselves down and sell ourselves short. So don't do that.

Me:	In addition to *Weeds*, you've also done quite a bit of episodic work on various television shows. I know that people now call specifically for you. How has that changed your life?
Hemky:	I still audition, and most of the casting directors already know me and I know them. They've seen me for nine years. But it's a great experience when they call and want to know my availability. Before it was like, okay, can you get me into the room? Now, they go, "Hemky, I want to offer you this role." That's nice!
	The New Normal was like that. I didn't have to audition. They called, they offered the role, and I was like, "Cool." Then of course, the next day I went to another audition. You have no idea how many name actors you see in auditions. You will always audition until the day you die. There's times when you will get offered roles, but don't also believe that because you get to a certain point, that things get easier.
Me:	How do you handle the down times between jobs, or if you get close and you don't get something? How do you handle all of that?
Hemky:	Before I got married and had a kid? (Laughter)
Me:	Before you got married and had a kid.
Hemky:	I play golf. I train, take classes, keep active.
	Keep yourself active. Just that, keep yourself active and save money for the down times, because you might make a lot of money— and I made this mistake, that oh, my God, the money came. Oh, my God, I can buy myself this and buy myself that... Then I'm broke again. Just find something you like that's peaceful for you. For me, it was golf. I play golf with all my friends. Now my down time is my family, between gigs or even during the gigs, I got Georgie and Jessie

	at home. My wife and son, they keep me centered now.
Me:	So you created a life outside of the acting to keep you sane.
Hemky:	Oh, definitely.
Me:	How important is that?
Hemky:	I'd say it's the most important thing of all, because otherwise you will go insane, especially in this town.
Me:	Is producing something you want to do, because you had the producing soap operas back in the Dominican Republic? Would you want to move into producing or directing, in addition to acting?
Hemky:	Definitely. I even have a company called Mako Films.
Me:	Are you working on anything now for that company?
Hemky:	Right now, I'm just trying to get material. My wife and I, we're writing a pilot for the story of our life.
Me:	What is it that you think separates the people who create longevity in their career from the people who are just a flash in the pan?
Hemky:	Wow, that's an interesting question. I could give you this in just a simple example. A lot of people come here to LA for pilot season and say, "You know what, I'm going to be a star in three months." They put in all their energy and then three months comes, and nothing happens. Okay, then one year, two years. They don't give themselves time. You have to just keep going, because the beauty about what we do— I could be ninety years old and you need a ninety year-old actor. You've just got to keep fighting, and love what you do, find yourself, and make enough money for you to live.

I'm lucky that I live out of acting now. I don't live like a rock star, but I pay my bills. Before, that wasn't the case. I couldn't pay my bills. Now I pay my bills and I have a family. Just believe in yourself, not to the point where you think that you're the biggest thing on the block, but just keep at it. Keep fighting, keep fighting for what you believe and what you love. If you love acting, and you love directing, and you love writing, just keep doing it and don't let anybody say, " No, you're not good enough."

Who are they to tell me I'm not good enough? I might not be right for that part. They might not see me as the part. I might be perfect for the part but they might not see me as the part. So? If that would be the case, I should have quit five, six times ago. I should have quit when I got burned out in New York. I should have quit when I came here and I couldn't get anything. I should have quit after the campaign failed and I got depressed. I should have quit even after *Weeds,* because my role was so memorable, it was hard for people to see me differently for a second. I should have quit then, too. I should have quit when I met my wife and had my kid.

You have to do what you have to do, but just don't let anybody— especially yourself— don't give yourself an "until this day." You crazy? Come on. That's insane. That, for me, is crazy. And not believing in yourself? That's crazy. Believe in yourself and go for it, man.

Jesse Heiman,
Character Actor, Go Daddy Campaign Star, World's Greatest Extra, Pop Culture Icon

Although you may not know his name, you've seen Jesse in countless films and TV shows over the years, often in the background.

In fact, Jesse has been dubbed the World's Greatest Extra, with a huge fan following playing a "Where's Waldo" kind of game with ever project he's been in.

His popularity spawned a YouTube video sensation produced by some Swedish fans highlighting him in most of the shows he's appeared in.

However, Jesse has also been cast in a number of legitimate speaking roles for many films and programs such as *Entourage* and *The Mindy Project*, and featured as the star of numerous commercial campaigns, including the famous Go Daddy Super Bowl spot that catapulted him to instant pop culture icon stardom.

A Texas transplant, Jesse has twelve solid years of industry experience, and he serves as an inspiration to anyone following their dream.

Me: Did you always want to be an actor?

Jesse: I thought I was going to be a writer or a producer, which I still want to, but I didn't realize that my potential could be in front of the camera. I thought I was only good for behind the camera activities.

Me: Then how did you discover that you wanted to be an actor? What were the events leading up to you saying, "I'm moving to LA to be an actor?"

Jesse: It just happened. It was really just when I started doing extra work. When I lost my first job I started to do extra work, and they kept calling for me to do more. I thought, "Oh, that's cool." They wanted to see me in front of the camera so I thought, well, if there is a demand to see me, I should try to be better at it.

I was working on sets with these amazing actors and I wanted to be just like them. I wanted to work with them and be on the same level with them.

I find that learning on set is the best tool. People frown upon doing extra work. They say, "Oh, you shouldn't do extra work, it's going to take away from your acting." That's b.s. People should encourage actors to do extra work because it gives you so much experience, you get to learn so much about how the industry works, where your place is in industry, how to respect people, and how to just enjoy working on a set.

How do you enjoy working on set? You have to know there's going to be long hours of downtime, long hours of just standing and walking and doing crosses and doing the same action over and over and over again, and it's all to get two seconds of film time. It's a lot of work. And that's just the first scene of the day!

Me: What was the very first speaking role you, and was it a film or television show?

Jesse: It was TV show. It was before I even had an agent. I was working regularly as an extra on this show called *Maybe It's Me* and they kept bringing me back as part of the chess club, or part of the nerds. Then they brought me in one day just to talk to me and they said, "We want to give you a part, we want to give you some lines," and, "Do you have any experience with that?" I said no, and they said, "Oh, we'll give you a chance."

             The director had me come in without an audition and just do it. It was amazing.

Me: Did that lead to other things, that one line? Did that directly lead to more work or was it still a constant

Jesse: I don't know how many people actually saw that

episode, besides my parents and people that I told to watch it. I have no idea if someone watched it and said, "Hey this is great, let's give him a line and bring him into something else." But it started kind of the flow, it started making things come, feel like this is all worth something, it's all going to be something.

Then, even non-speaking parts— like when I was starting to show up in films— I was telling people for weeks, "Hey, go see Spider-Man! I think I might be in it," and they would say, "You're not in Spider-Man. What are you talking about? You're not an actor, we never see you. You're never there." Then all my friends went to go see Spider-Man and they were like, "What the heck? What's he doing there? Wow! He's really in it! Amazing!" But there was still kind of skepticism. It was like, "What are you doing? You're not talking, you're just a moving tree or prop. You're not a real actor."

Me: You've been in the industry for 12 years, and needless to say, because of the YouTube sensation— that montage of you called *The World's Greatest Extra*— then the Go Daddy Super Bowl commercial, your life now is dramatically different.

Jesse: It's similar but it's not the same as it was when I started of course. I'm doing a lot less extra work now and I'm not stressing about not having work. Like, there was downtime when I was working as an extra, I would be like, "I don't know when my next job is, I don't know when my next pay check is coming in." A lot of the time I was living pay check to pay check, living month to month, and it's really fun now because I don't know what's coming next, but it's always going to be something awesome or great.

Me: Yeah, so obviously everybody knows that this Go Daddy commercial blew you up pretty huge.

Jesse:	This is the biggest one. This is my breakthrough, yeah.
Me:	But you had done a lot of actual legit work. In addition to extra work on Spider-Man and other films, you had some lines, actual roles, in shows like, *Entourage* , *The Mindy Project, Monk,* and you were recurring on *Chuck.*
Jesse:	Yeah.
Me:	A lot of people don't know that you'd actually done quite a bit of commercial work. You did a commercial campaign for Vonage, and more recently, Prego.
Jesse:	Yeah.
Me:	Can you talk about being a steadily working actor and, now, being so big that you've been on the *Tonight Show* a couple of times, most recently as a correspondent for the Oscars?
Jesse:	You start feeling really good about yourself when you're working on a commercial. I had just done the first *Transformers* movie with Michael Bay, and he really liked me. He like put me in this shot that I never saw in the movie, so it never made the cut. But he had me running towards a helicopter.

And then I booked the Vonage commercial and on the day of the shoot, production called from *Transformers* and said, "We need you today! They're doing a reshoot for *Transformers!*" They said if I don't show, I probably was not going to be in the film. I was like, "Well I can't go I'm shooting a commercial," so I had to turn it down. I did the commercial and it was successful.

Two years later I did *Transformers 3* and Michael Bay he demanded me for *Transformers 2,* but I wasn't available. So I worked on *Transformers 3,* and he put me right in the center of a shot, walking by Shia LaBeouf and John Malkovich is doing something, and you can see me dead on, and everybody is like, "Wow this is awesome."

It's stuff like that— even if you turn someone down they still bring you back— that kind of stuff is amazing to me. That is worth way more than the money... I mean it's cool getting checks, money is awesome, of course, but getting the call to come work for someone again is great.

I also did two spots for Metro PCS. They dumped me in the tank of goo. That one didn't play that much, but the one where I got hung upside down, it played a bunch. That was two separate commercials and I got two separate paychecks, and two separate stunt bumps because I did stunts. And there are the Pringle ads that I'm in right now currently, that are still running, I'm still getting money from that, and that's amazing.

Me: Do you recommend for people who are starting out to pursue commercial work in addition to extra work?

Jesse: Yes. And you can start doing commercial work as an extra. You make more money on a commercial. There are companies in town that just do commercials background casting, and every day they have, like, five commercials going on. In a commercial the background rate's, like, two to three hundred dollars. So I mean, it's almost the principal rate. My rate is, like, six hundred, or something, for a one day of work as a principle.

Sometimes commercials for extras could be a short day, you don't have to be there the whole day. Or there'll be multiple days where they'll need you, two of those that will pay for your week.

Me:	You had a fan in Sweden who did a video compilation of you as the "World's Greatest Extra" which kind of catapulted you into this cult following, an iconic—
Jesse:	Yeah, guys from Sweden, they made the *World's Greatest Extra* video and it got me on the *Tonight Show* as a guest within a month of it being online, which is amazing. Then, when the Go Daddy ad aired, they were really proud of me and they said, well let's bring him back on. They actually had me on before the Oscars show. They had me on with Bar Refaeli to recreate the kiss with her. Jay wanted to do the kiss with her, but he closed his eyes and when he opened them, I was the one who ended up kissing Jay.
Me:	That was really funny.
Jesse:	Yeah, then he wanted me to go to the Vanity Fair party after the Academy Awards to be on the red carpet as a correspondent for them. And the coolest part of it was the majority of stars knew who I was. I didn't have to introduce myself to them. They'd seen the commercial.
Me:	Now there is a documentary film crew doing a film about your life? How did that come about?
Jesse:	I've had a few other opportunities for people to do a documentary but they haven't been able to get the funds together. But these guys from Kentucky came out and they said they wanted to do a full feature-length documentary about me, and I said that sounds cool. They talked to my agent and my manager, and everybody seemed excited, so they came out a couple of months ago and we shot a trailer. Now there's a Kickstarter campaign.
Me:	You've also had some other incredible opportunities come up. I understand that you're working on a potential book deal?

Jesse:	Yes. I think we're waiting to find out if there is interest beyond the publisher, or beyond the agents, or something. It's funny because I started out wanting to be a writer
Me:	And you're trying to develop a series around you? Is that correct? Your manager and your agent and you are trying to come up with something? Is that right?
Jesse:	Well I'm writing something with my friends. We're going to try and shoot trailer for it.
Me:	How can actors be more proactive and more productive in their careers if they don't have representation? Especially people who are just starting out?
Jesse:	Just have patience. Just get yourself out there, do what I did, go be an extra, or if you want to be in the theater, go work at a theater. And be prepared... If you're out there, you'll be seen by someone. YouTube and Funny or Die— put yourself on camera.
	Just be professional. Don't come here thinking this is an easy job. Be professional, be on time, be consistent.
	And roll with the punches. It sounds so cliché, but just roll with the punches and just do whatever they ask of you, because it's all going to be worth it.
	Yesterday and the day before, I was working on a promo for a YouTube award show. And the coolest part about it was, I was number one on the caller sheet, and the whole day, for two days I was the number one person there with most responsibility, the most lines, the most action and I handled it, like, no problem. I just did whatever they had me do— put on all these crazy outfits... I loved having that much responsibility and just got to go to town with it.
Me:	What's the biggest challenge in starting out?

Jesse:	I would say it's just finding the time to do things. A lot of the time life will get in the way, but if you want to do this, you gotta go to class, you gotta make sure you have time to go to work, time to sleep, you gotta eat got to... I mean just manage your time wisely.
	And just focus on you. Make others happy, but make sure you're happy, too. If you're not happy with what's going on, you can take some time to think about it. Whatever you need to do to let yourself feel happy, and if at any point you feel like you need a break, go take a break. You'll have plenty of time in your career to progress.
Me:	Has it been a difficult journey for you in certain respects?
Jesse:	Oh yeah, absolutely. It's difficult for everyone.
Me:	And how do you handle those kinds of stresses?
Jesse:	I just deal with it. At this point I know that it'll all work out. I just roll with the punches and I know it'll be fine.
Me:	Any last words?
Jesse:	Thank you very much and I hope you all have beautiful dreams and you follow them.

Spotlight

Allison Burnett,
Writer, Producer, Director

I first met Allison when I was in high school. He was my
S.A.T. tutor in a program called the Princeton Review, and by far,
the coolest person anyone could ask for in a verbal tutor. I liked
him right away, and not just because he was a writer, but because he
was, and still is, warm and approachable, and he holds everyone to
a high standard so that they may do their best.

Now he is a highly successful writer of novels, such as *Death
by Sunshine, A House Beautiful, Christopher: A Tale of Seduction,* and
Undiscovered Gyrl, which he recently adapted for the screen and
directed, and stars Britt Robertson, Christian Slater, Justin Long,
and Martin Sheen. Allison also wrote and directed one of my
favorite indie films, *Red Meat,* starring Lara Flynn Boyle and John
Slattery.

I've chose to spotlight Allison because, as a respected writer,
he is masterful with the economy of language, and answers these
interview questions honestly and directly. He tells you exactly how
it is.

Me: What do you look for in an audition?

Allison: An epiphany I experienced while directing
Undiscovered Gyrl is that the actor who wins the role
(presuming that he is physically right for it) is the one
who relates and understands it best. The one who
resonates with it most deeply. This is not something
that the actor can think his way to, but rather it is a
product of his life experience, his sensibility, his very
essence.

Me: How important are prior credits versus training?

Allison: In Utopia, the best actor for the role would win
it every time. But in the real world, there is huge
pressure to go with names whenever possible. It's
the simple reality of film financing. As for training,

the only training that matters to me is actual working experience.

Me: What are some factors that actors may not know that either gets them the jobs or keeps them from getting it?

Allison: That ninety percent of the time, they have no chance for the role before they even begin to read, based solely on their physicality, or some other aspect of them, that is out of their control. An actor can rail at the injustice of this, or he can use it as a source of relaxation and comfort: "Getting this role is out of my hands, so I might as well relax and have fun and give the best reading I can."

As a director, I am looking for the actor who brings an understanding to the role that transcends the lines being read. The actor who inhabits the part. In order to do this, the actor must be relaxed, connected. It's crucial that he sees himself as an equal to those in a position to hire him. He must not come in hat in hand, but as a fellow artist who knows that if we do not work together on this project then perhaps the next one. An actor who comes in nervous and insecure and overeager is finished before he opens his mouth.

Me: What's your personal casting process?

Allison: I love to stop the actors while they are reading and give them direction. The best actors can take notes and immediately implement them. When the director stops you, don't freeze up and feel criticized. In fact, it's always a good sign when a director does this. It means you have a chance for the part. It means you're worth the investment of his precious time.

Me: What's your biggest challenge when casting a project?

Allison:	Balancing the importance of getting a great actor for the role with getting a famous name for the role. When you get both, it's a dream come true.
Me:	What's the biggest challenge in directing a newcomer as opposed to a star?
Allison:	Film acting is brutally hard. The actor often has a camera stuck right in his face, lights everywhere, a crew staring at him, and with the clock ticking, has to make written lines sound as though he'd said them before— all the while matching his gestures and timing to those of his previous takes. This is a hardcore craft. It takes instinctive intelligence and fierce concentration. It's very hard for a newcomer to walk onto a set and do this. Working with a talented star is a joy because they do it with breathtaking ease.
Me:	What should actors never do out there?
Allison:	Never compare yourself to others, grow bitter, feel entitled to work, stop taking acting class, get tattoos, cheat on your lovers and spouses during a shoot, surrender to drugs and alcohol, have children unless they you put them before your work, or get bad plastic surgery.
Me:	What should they never do with you?
Allison:	Cop attitude, get defensive, be late, make excuses, and change lines without asking first.
Me:	What do you love about your job?
Allison:	Once you get it right once, it's there forever. It's an incredible feeling to drive home after a day's work and know that you got what you wanted in the can, and that nothing short of the sun exploding is going to make it go away.

Me:	What do you love about actors?
Allison:	Their courage, emotional depth, openness, and freaky instinctive intelligence.
Me:	What's your biggest pet peeve?
Allison:	I have two. Narcissism and improvisation.

Studies show that even a non-actor when put into the limelight will start to demonstrate narcissistic symptoms. Psychiatrists call it situational narcissism. It's very hard to resist, but an artist must resist it at all costs, because in the end it will destroy him. Every artist should live from the perspective that he is an attention-seeking monster, seeking to fill a vast void inside him with adulation from outside— and then work very hard to be otherwise. It's a daily struggle, but in the end it will make him a better artist and person.

Ninety-five percent of an actor's improvisation is terrible. It can be a great tool in rehearsal to help the actor relax and find his character, but in an actual performance it's woeful. It's repetitious, obvious, and bad: "Are you talking to me? Are you talking to me?" A sophisticated audience member can spot it a mile off. It immediately calls attention to itself and interrupts the dream of the story. It's also deeply insulting to the writer that the actor thinks the crap that occurs to him off the top of his head is better than what it took the writers months to craft. If the lines, as written, are so terrible that you can improve them by improvising, then you shouldn't have taken the job in the first place.

Me:	Tell me an inspiring Cinderella story.
Allison:	Britt Robertson was my first choice for the lead role of Katie in *Undiscovered Gyrl*. Due to an idiotic

mistake, the offer of the role to Britt was delayed by four days. By the time it finally came in, Britt had said yes to a small role in a big Hollywood movie—one which she would never have taken over Katie. The schedules conflicted. Nothing could be done. I moved on, heartbroken, without her. I cast someone else, whom I was forced to fire a week before shooting. A mad search ensued for another Katie. Two days later, I received a letter from Britt, telling me how heartbroken she had been to lose the role, and that she felt that she was meant to play it, and that if we were willing to work around her schedule, she would give everything she had to play Katie. I called her back in to read again just to make sure she meant what she said. She read brilliantly. It was a scheduling and financial nightmare to make the film work with Britt in the role, but it was the best choice I could have made. She is perfection.

Me: What's the best career advice you could give to someone just starting out?

Allison: There is no such thing as a happy actor. If there is anything else you can do in life and stay sane, do that instead. If you have no choice, then give acting everything you have. The day you quit acting is the day you never were one.

Me: What's the best acting or audition advice you can give?

Allison: Relax, have fun, be yourself, the people in the room are your equals.

Me: What's the best career advice you have for the seasoned actor?

Allison: Don't be afraid to age. The passage of time will lead to wonderful new roles.   Imagine if, say, Burt Reynolds or Tony Curtis had shed their toupees and been unafraid of passing time. Both gifted actors, they might have had brilliant third acts to their careers.

Me: What's the biggest myth or misconception people have about the industry?

Allison: That it's who you know. This is absolute crap. Who you know might open a door or two, but you have to deliver. Again and again.

Me: How has the industry changed in the last ten years that make it harder for actors, directors, writers, etc.? And what makes it easier?

Allison: Salaries are way down. Quotes don't matter. The studios and networks are squeezing the talent for every nickel. On the other hand, the digital revolution and the growth of cable means that there are far more jobs available.

Paul Smith,
Top Headshot Photographer

Originally from Australia, Paul Smith has been voted number one Backstage Readers Choice headshot photographer four years in a row. And with clients like Abrams, APA, CAA, ICM, and William Morris/Endeavor, to name only a few, you know the quality has to be top-notch. But you can see that for yourself just by looking through his masterful portfolio of work.

Being that the headshot is the number one most important marketing tool an actor must have, I found it obvious that I include some insights from the best that Los Angeles has to offer.

Me: So, Paul, what process does the top Hollywood headshot photographer have?

Paul: Well, first of all, thank you. It's truly amazing to be regarded as the top headshot photographer in Hollywood. I love what I do and I worked hard to get here. I started shooting actors in my Hollywood garage thirteen years ago and just kept on going. Every person that walks in the door brings in a different energy and it keeps me on my toes artistically to capture that. As an artist myself, it's important to stay fresh and not have a formula. I don't want people to look at my shots and say, "Oh, Paul Smith shot that." I want them to look at my work and be captivated by the actor's energy.

Me: What do you think sets you apart from other photographers?

Paul: Again, it's not having a formula. I listen to my clients. I feed off of them and help guide them throughout the shoot without being overbearing or intimidating.

Me: Without revealing your "secret sauce," how do you like to work with actors?

Paul: First, I ask my actors to come prepared. I give them
          "homework" to help them get them out of their head
          and into their gut. Ninety percent is preparation and
          ten percent is letting go.

          So many actors have "headshot baggage" from
          spending a fortune and not achieving what they
          need or require for this business. I ask those actors
          what they did to prepare for the shoot and most reply
          with talk about getting their hair cut or choosing
          clothes. That gives me an idea of why their shoots
          might be unsuccessful. Concentrating only on the
          exterior and not the internal. You have to be specific
          in what you are trying to say. How you are trying to
          market yourself. You don't just show up at auditions
          thinking, "You know, I will just be myself, forget
          about lines or what my intention is." Being yourself is
          important and it will be the thing that sets you apart
          from the thousands out here trying to do the same
          thing, however, the *intention* behind it is key.

Me: What's the most important thing actors should know
          when looking for a headshot photographer? And
          what are some red flags?

Paul: You should feel comfortable with the photographer. I
          want actors to look at my website and be captivated
          by what they see. To keep coming back to it because
          it's what they want to achieve. I feel that the actors in
          my work reflect that ease or comfort level that was felt
          during their photo shoot.

          Red flags… If the photographer asks you to get
          naked… no, but seriously. Also, if your representation
          requires you to go to that photographer. Hey listen,
          I have built a great reputation with a lot of industry
          folks over the years and I know that there are some
          managers and agents who strongly urge their clients
          to come my way. I appreciate that. But there are
          also some dodgy dealings going on with other

	photographers and agents. Kick-backs and so forth. I don't work that way. My work speaks for itself.

Me: What's the biggest misconception about what makes a good headshot?

Paul: The biggest misconception about what make a good headshot is too much attention to the little things. I had one actress come in and change nails for each look. Casting is not looking at your nails in the pics, trust me. They are looking at your energy.

Me: What's the biggest misconception about what makes a good photographer?

Paul: How many celebrities they have shot... I know some mediocre photographers that have a lot of famous faces on their websites. Maybe they are friends with them. Maybe they've worked a deal with the publicist. Just don't let famous faces fool you. Look at the photography, as well.

Me: What's the biggest obstacle you've encountered as a headshot photographer?

Paul: I have been lucky enough not to encounter a big obstacle. You bring in what you put out there. I have been pretty lucky to have had some amazing actors to work with. Every once in a while I get a doozy, but most of the time, I know it going in... So, I just work with it. I am not changing the world. I am taking headshots.

Me: What should every newcomer know when booking and showing up for a shoot?

Paul: How to listen to your gut. Be professional, be on time and courteous. These things will get you far in life and in the business.

Me: What should actors never do during a shoot?

Paul:	Drink alcohol. Seriously, had one actress show up on my set almost drunk. She thought drinking would relax her. She looked cross-eyed in most of the shots.
Me:	What can actors do to stand out?
Paul:	Be themselves. Nobody else is you. I pride myself on creating a safe, relaxed environment for actors to come and hang out. Just be yourself and let me capture it.
Me:	Do you confer with agents and managers when shooting their talent?
Paul:	Yes, I always have my door open. Some agents and managers even come to the shoots with their clients, but I wouldn't recommend that for everyone. The more info I know about a client, the better, so if an agent or manager wants to confer, then of course. I don't want the call: "Hey we love your work and your shots, unfortunatley this is just not how we market our client." That tells me that the actor never conferred with their reps— the most important people to do so with. And then they end up with pictures that won't do them justice.
Me:	Being that "type" is everything in a headshot, how do you help actors define that for themselves?
Paul:	I give my actors homework. However, I am not the person sending them out on auditions. If they're a newbie, I have been around long enough to guide them in a certain direction that will help them find representation with the shots I get for them. But if the actor has been around the block a little, then I expect them to know what kind of roles they should be landing and how to get a picture to project that.

It's really not up to me to "market" my actor. I am just there to help them, be part of their package to |

help them with that. I do try to steer my clients in a positive direction that I think will help them market themselves the best way they can. Some people are not ready to see the reality in themselves, though. Sometimes it takes going through some time out here, acting classes, casting workshops, and auditions to see what you are good at and the roles that you consistently land. And just being real with yourself. Sometimes the only obstacles I have are people who are their own obstacles.

Me: Any final thoughts or advice?

Paul: Don't get your nickers in a twist over headshots. Yes, they are part of your calling card, but remember, YOU are the calling card. Let that come through and the rest will take care of itself.

* * *

To see Paul's work or book a session,
visit **www.PaulSmithPhotography.com**

Clear Talent Group, L.A.
Young People's Department
Bonnie Ventis, Jody Alexander, Philip Marcus

All the agents of CTG's Young People's Department are some of the most highly respected agents in the industry, representing such notable stars as *Modern Family's* Rico Rodriguez and *Napoleon Dynamite's* Efren Ramirez, to name just a couple.

For parents of child actors, or for the young people themselves, the advice they offer is invaluable.

Me: What holds actors back from getting work?

Bonnie: Not being prepared, not being marketable. Having unrealistic expectations of the industry. Also, lack of knowledge as to how to audition.

Me: What do you look for in headshots?

Bonnie: The actor needs to look like their photo, we also look for something interesting or compelling going on within the actor— a subtext.

Me: How important is acting training for children, and what kind of training do you look for?

Jody: Training is critical. This is a very competitive industry. There are a lot of actors and not nearly enough auditions (opportunities) for all.

When an actor does have an audition he/she needs to make a positive lasting impression. Training with a reputable acting teacher will help with this process. Continuing to work on the craft of acting is a must!

Me: Why is it easier to break into the business as a child?

Jody: A three year old who is just starting out isn't expected to have the training and the resume that a thirty-three year old should have. No one is born being a member of SAG/AFTRA, and when a casting director has to justify why a non-union actor was hired by them on a union job, it is easier to do so when it is a small child who is cute and natural.

Me: Aside from always being extremely busy, what does your typical day look like?

Jody: Part of what is so wonderful about our industry is we don't have typical days! As we sit at our desks first thing in the morning we never know what breakdowns are going to come out that day. Who will have an audition? Who will get a callback? Who will get a book a job? What casting director will respond to e-mail pitches and what casting director will respond to a friendly phone call. Yes, we may continue to work on a big contract and yes we usually have representation appointments but even these are fun and we never know how these will work out.

Me: What's the biggest advice you can give to a seasoned young actor or parent?

Philip: I would sum it up in one word: "Communication." It is key to communicate with your agent and/or manager. We need to know when you are running late to an audition before casting calls to complain that you are late. We need to know before an audition that you are not comfortable with the material. We need to know before we pitch that you are not available to make an audition, etc. Communication is absolutely key.

Me: What's the biggest challenge child actors face?

Philip: I can name a few different things: 1. Parents that are over-bearing and put unnecessary pressure on their children to succeed. Parents should support, but not pressure their children; 2. Finding the balance between this business and leading a normal child's life. We encourage going to birthday parties, school field trips, extracurricular activities, BUT, you must communicate with your agent when you are not available; 3. Always comparing yourself to other children in the casting office waiting room— be your own self and do not worry about everyone else. Focus on what you are going to do to leave a positive image with the casting director.

Me: How different is the business now compared to, maybe five years ago?

Philip: On the negative side, the industry has become so over-loaded with child actors from all fifty states. Kids form out of town pour into LA with a parent by the thousands.

          The positive side is that more and more theatrical casting directors are willing to look at audition links from out of town kids. If they like what they see, then they will schedule a callback meeting and the child will have to come to LA.

          I wouldn't be surprised if in the near future, casting directors begin hosting Skype sessions for out of town talent. Also, everything is electronic, sucha s casting via websites, so the cost of printing headshots has gone down a lot.

www.ingramcontent.com/pod-product-compliance
Lightning Source LLC
Chambersburg PA
CBHW060017100426
42740CB00010B/1505